TAMING YOUR TEMPER

A WORKBOOK FOR INDIVIDUALS, COUPLES, AND GROUPS

BY NATHANIEL DAVID SMITH, MA, NCC, LPC-S

Author's note: I urge any reader with serious problems (e.g., frequently violent, suicidal thoughts, homicidal plans) to seek professional help in addition to (or instead of) using the workbook. If you are having dangerous impulses, intrusive and aggressive thoughts, or ideas of self-harm, please seek immediate professional help.

All of the client stories have been altered to protect the confidentiality of the client's.

This book may be purchased for business or promotional use or for special sales. For sales information or permissions to reprint this text or the material within, contact the publisher at:

Mental Health Classes, LLC
1101 E Plano Parkway
Suite F
Plano, TX 75075
To order more books: https://www.createspace.com/3948640
www.nathanielsmithcounselor.com
(972) 423-0901

ISBN 13: 978-0-9856681-0-5

Printed in the U.S.A.

Praise for Taming Your Temper

We all need tools for anger management. The simpler, more effective, and user-friendly those tools are—the better. Nathaniel Smith makes efficient use of the pages in this workbook. He wastes no space on useless concepts or unnecessary rambling. Instead, he calls upon Cognitive Behavior Therapy as a solid, trusted foundation upon which to build a series of valuable ideas. He illustrates those ideas with colorful stories and offers easy-to-understand exercises which help the reader practice and solidify their learning.

This workbook is comprehensive. It starts with helping you understand where anger originates, teaches you how to handle anger in various aspects of your life, and gives you tools for preventing unhealthy expressions of anger. It teaches us all what we wish we had learned when we were ten, twelve, or fifteen. Nathaniel Smith is giving us the chance to catch up, to keep up, and to get ahead. He's teaching us something he already knows: Anger Management can be fun, and it can help you improve every part of your life. It's not too late to Tame Your Temper.

—**Pamela Milam, MA, LPC, NCC, BCC Dallas Texas**

Nathaniel Smith is a counselor who knows a good deal about the effects of unchecked anger through his work with clients as a Certified Anger Resolution Therapist, Member of the Texas Council on Family Violence, and through his Texas Department of Criminal Justice accredited Battering Intervention and Prevention Program. Learning to manage anger and self soothe is an important tool in building and maintaining meaningful relationships both in our personal lives and in the workplace. News reports provide further evidence on a daily basis that confirm the importance of this work. Taming Your Temper is an invaluable contribution towards this endeavor.

—**Linda W. McCune, M.S., LPC-S Dallas Texas**

There are many books written dealing with Anger Management, but none as comprehensive as this book. The book covers all the necessary topics from what causes anger, faulty beliefs about anger, unhealthy vs. healthy responses to anger, and how to safely deal with anger. Nathaniel uses Cognitive Behavior Therapy as his foundation for teaching anger management. The book is full of stories and simple, easy-to-follow exercises to guide clients through their journey in dealing with anger. The simplicity of this book is its greatest point. The book is well organized and well written. Nathaniel is more than qualified to write this book. I know that he truly has empathy and it shows in his work with his clients. He has a passion for this subject.

—**Steven R. Jackman, M.S., LPC, BIPP Coordinator, Dallas Texas**

Nathaniel Smith's magical ability to connect with clients is evident not only by the unusually high compliance rate, but also by the glowing feedback I receive directly from my patients. Since 2008, Nathaniel has been an invaluable resource to our family medicine practice. He is a gifted counselor who has successfully engaged so many of my patients, assisting them with a variety of emotional hardships. Nathaniel earned our trust not only as a successful counselor, but also highly dependable diagnostic resource, helping us unravel a spectrum of complex and frequently intermingled psychological disorders. He's been integral to my practice, and I'm confident that his methods will benefit many individuals and couples.

—**Aaron P. Segal, M.D., Family Medicine Plano, TX**

BOOKS AND WORKBOOKS

TAMING YOUR TEMPER
A WORKBOOK FOR INDIVIDUALS, COUPLES, AND GROUPS

Are you tired of the ruined relationships that result from your angry and destructive feelings?
Taming Your Temper: A Workbook for Individuals, Couples, and Groups contains 36 concrete strategies that teach how to express anger in healthy ways. Taming Your Temper is a necessary element for anyone wishing to curtail their own aggression and live a healthier life. This book is used in all Temper Tamers programs and anger management groups.

Visit this website to buy: http://bit.ly/19T1flJ

TEMPER TAMERS
A PROGRAM FOR GROUPS BASED ON TAMING YOUR TEMPER: TEACHERS MANUAL

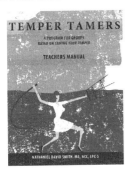

If you are a life coach, clergy member, mental health professional, probation officer or anyone who wishes to facilitate an effective anger management group, then this guide is for you. Used in conjunction with the Temper Tamers Certification video series, the Temper Tamers Facilitator Guide will offer teachers a way to provide a well-rounded and holistic approach when helping group members to control their rage and explosive anger.

Visit this website to buy: http://bit.ly/19hwE4r

ONLINE MEMBERSHIP

Becoming a Temper Tamers online member means that you or your organization can get ongoing training that exceeds that of the initial certification program. This includes access to a wide range of resources that can be used to complement the effective techniques taught by the program.
Membership Is Available In Three Levels:

Free Temper Tamers Membership will allow you to get a free preview of the materials available in the membership program.

With **Silver Level Membership**, certified individuals and organizations will bte given access to the exclusive Temper Tamers marketing package and automated forms for intake and referrals. These forms allow for completion on a computer, eliminating the need to print them out until such time as physical form placement in a client file is required. This makes it easier for your organization to complete any monthly referral reports with ease.

The **Gold Level Membership** provides certified individuals and organizations with access to both the Temper Tamers marketing package and automated forms for intake and referrals. In addition, Gold membership also includes the delivery of an exclusive training video each month. The video will increase the effectiveness of your teaching, thereby increasing your value to your Temper Tamers class participants.

Visit this website to buy: http://bit.ly/GVouVB

Contents

Setting Boundaries   117

Taming Your Temper: The Life Plan   151

Acknowledgments

I would like to express my gratitude to the many people who saw me through this book; to all those who provided support, talked things over, read, wrote, offered comments, allowed me to quote their remarks and assisted in the editing, proofreading, and design.

I want to thank Pamela Milam who has been a friend and colleague for many years. Her guidance and support heavily influenced this project.

I would like to thank my wife and the rest of my family, who supported and encouraged me in spite of all the time it took me away from them.

Introduction

This book will not teach you that anger is bad. My goal is not to eliminate your anger or make you never feel angry again. Even if I had the power to do that, I would not try because I'm here to tell you: Anger is normal! It's a natural human emotion we all share. Does that surprise you? Let me tell you about me and my wife. We have a great relationship, but do we have conflict? Absolutely. Do we get angry? You bet. But—and this "but" is really the most important point I can make—*we do not let our anger escalate into aggression.* We don't take out our anger in verbally or physically abusive ways. We try not to lose our self-control. How do we manage to feel angry but not act out our anger? Through this book I will explain to you and anyone who has suffered the havoc, chaos, desperation, and despair of angry explosions how to get angry without acting out that anger.

Here's the bottom line: You can't change a feeling, but you can change a thought. And once you learn how to change a thought, you can change your behavior. A fancy name for this is cognitive behavior therapy. It just means that although you may experience feelings of anger your entire life, you do not have to be at the mercy of those feelings. You can learn to act in healthier ways, to cut down on aggression, to live in a calmer, more serene way.

You can learn to tame your temper.

I know you can because I've helped hundreds of clients in my counseling practice succeed in managing their anger.

Maybe you're reading this book with resentment or reluctance because some professional suggested it. Or maybe you're being forced by a court mandate to give it a try. Possibly you're reading it because you know your life is in a shambles but you have no idea why. Whatever the reason, I want you to know that your problem does not stem from anger. Chances are very good that your true underlying issue, the emotions causing such extreme turmoil for you, is pain and fear.

Take my client Alex, who first came to see me for depression. He owned his own telecommunications company that at one time was booming. He and his wife lived a luxurious lifestyle, spending a lot of the millions Alex made. When the business began floundering, he started to experience tremendous economic pressure. Frustrated and hopeless, he exploded in anger that often spiraled out of control. Realizing that his wife was spending as if they still had the same income, he put her on a tight allowance. He constantly chided her, complaining that she was selfish and that she never listened to him. He grilled her on every penny she spent, even if it was for necessities such as the children's clothing or groceries. He was big on throwing things like the remote control and slamming doors so hard they would splinter. Finally, he had a major temper tantrum and kicked his foot right through the screen of a $15,000 television set.

After delving into Alex's depression, I determined that he had major anger management issues. I began gradually connecting those dots for him. Once he could see how angry he was over his company's collapse, he recognized that he was taking it out on his wife and behaving irrationally. Today, I'm happy to report his business has turned around and his marriage is intact.

I could tell you dozens of similar stories from people who have come to me suffering with anger issues. Their histories may be different, but the same problem lies at their source: uncontrollable anger wrecking their lives.

I have only compassion and care for my clients, no matter how badly they've behaved, because I can see through their angry swaggering to their inner suffering. So I never try to make them feel guilty for what they've done, and I do not want you to feel guilt either. I know you're a good person who's done some things you regret. So let's work together, step by step, to help restore your life to sanity.

Through the years I have developed a series of concrete strategies, questionnaires, tips, and exercises that I assign clients over a period of weeks. I am happy to share them with you in the pages that follow.

I strongly recommend that you make a commitment to tackle at least two exercises a week for about 16 weeks. My approach—cognitive behavioral therapy—is not meant to take years. If you are willing to think through your thought patterns, which admittedly may be somewhat painful, and put a bit of time into filling out the questionnaires, I believe you will see improvement and feel relief by the end of four months.

There is an extraordinary power that comes from writing. As you complete each exercise, don't overthink your answers. Allow yourself to respond quickly and naturally, using each exercise as its own capsule lesson. But don't rush through the book, impatiently scribbling your answers in an effort to finish the entire workbook in one sitting. You may want to skip to the sections that interest you most—or seem the easiest!—but keep in mind that each exercise builds onto the next. While they may appear deceptively simple, the exercises are cumulative, so try to work sequentially on one section at a time. My experience tells me that you will build a stronger foundation for taming your temper if you go in order.

Each of the five chapters focuses on a different aspect of temper taming to bring you a keen awareness of where your anger comes from, what triggers your anger cycles, and how you can strengthen your self-control. When you have completed the book, you will have the knowledge and the tools to help you learn to calm down and tame your temper.

These effective exercises will not only help with anger, but with anxiety and depression as well. They hold a new mirror up to your inner and outer selves. By making slight adjustments, you can create a much more pleasant self-portrait. All you need is a pen—and the willingness to tame the temper that has been ruling and ruining your life. Welcome aboard and congratulations on taking the first step!

Author's note: *I urge any reader with serious problems (e.g., frequently violent, suicidal thoughts, homicidal plans) to seek professional help in addition to (or instead of) using the workbook. If you are having dangerous impulses, intrusive and aggressive thoughts, or ideas of self-harm, please seek immediate professional help.*

CHAPTER ONE

Understanding Your Anger

A 30-year-old client of mine named Mark ran a family gourmet food business with his older brother Andrew. They were continually in conflict over who was the more successful and what roles each played. Mark was responsible for the manufacturing side and his brother for marketing and financials. One day at the office, Andrew questioned Mark's decision to buy new equipment. The conversation got so heated that a fistfight broke out in front of the other employees. Mark has struggled for many years with controlling his anger. He takes things very personally and does not think before he reacts. And he does not understand why he keeps losing his temper—he only knows that if he doesn't do something soon, he is not only going to lose his company but his own brother.

What if I told you that whatever happens to you—your external circumstances—does not affect your feelings and behaviors? Would you be angry at me? Does that sound crazy? Would you ask "what does this guy know about all the hard knocks I've had?" It turns out that it doesn't matter one bit how hard your life has been: It's the way you *think* about what happens to you that makes the difference in how you feel and behave. You make these interpretations automatically, almost unconsciously as events take place. This is the idea behind cognitive therapy that can help you to identify, evaluate, and modify your thoughts to find relief. But first you need to figure out what underlying beliefs are holding you hostage.

When you were a child, you absorbed certain *core beliefs* about yourself, other people, and the world around you based on your interactions with family, friends, and events. Over time core beliefs took root: your particular ways of interpreting things. For example, let's say that when you were in kindergarten, you loved to draw pictures of family members using a series of circular shapes. Your teacher, however, insisted that you had to draw them as stick figures, like all the other kids did. You might have interpreted the teacher's words as a scolding, implying that there was something wrong with how you drew. You might have incorporated a core belief of "I'm inadequate" or "I'm not good enough." From then on, whenever anyone in any situation tells you, however gently, that you're not doing something the way it should be done or the way others do it, you will feel that little voice saying, "I'm inadequate, I'm not good enough." You literally only hear information that confirms your core belief, while ignoring or discounting information that suggests the contrary.

Core Beliefs give rise to **Rules, Attitudes, and Assumptions** that lead to **Automatic Thoughts.** These three elements—Rules, Attitudes, and Assumptions—combine to create our emotions and behavior. In this chapter I will show you how to understand the source of your anger by carefully leading you through three steps.

Step 1: Understand core beliefs, what they are, and where they come from. Your core beliefs are created early in life and determine how you view yourself and the world around you. Unhealthy core beliefs drive unhealthy automatic thoughts, prompting anger and frustration.

Step 2: Define the rules we make for ourselves, both good and bad. These rules grow out of our core beliefs and determine our behavior, especially in regard to anger.

Step 3: Become familiar with your automatic thoughts. Automatic thoughts can show up as mental images, self-talk, or habitual ways of perceiving situations as they arise. You will learn to categorize your automatic thoughts and understand how they create feelings and reactions.

CORE BELIEFS

Your core beliefs originated when you were a young child. It is through these beliefs that you form your perception of yourself and the world around you. You might have developed positive ideas about yourself such as "I'm special" or "I'm intelligent." But in this section, you examine your **Unhealthy Core Beliefs** ("I'm worthless" or "I'm bad"), which have a direct impact on your anger, and learn how to organize them into distinct categories.

Take a moment to look at the Unhealthy Core Beliefs below. Circle the ones that reflect the way you view yourself:

DEPENDENCE

I'm weak.

I'm not competent.

I'm incapable of solving my own problems.

I'm powerless to make changes.

I'm helpless.

FEAR OF INTIMACY

I'm always alone.

No one understands me.

People will always leave me.

I can't trust anyone.

I will always be rejected.

LOW SELF-ESTEEM

I'm not good enough.

I'm defective.

I'm worthless.

I'm bad.

I'm inadequate.

ADDICTION

I'm nothing.

I'm broken.

I'm toxic.

I have no control.

I can't function without substances.

I can't have fun without a substance.

I need my substance in order to be social.

AGGRESSION

I must be in control.

I must be more powerful.

I hate people.

I must win at all costs.

Other people don't matter.

ANXIETY

The world is a scary place.

I'm vulnerable.

Uncertainty is bad.

I'm out of control.

I'm likely to be hurt.

DEPRESSION

Life is hopeless.

I'll never be happy.

I don't deserve to live.

Depression is bad.

EXERCISE 1: CREATE YOUR HEALTHY CORE BELIEFS

Challenge your unhealthy core beliefs by completing this exercise. See the *Jumpstart Exercise to help you complete this exercise.*

1. Identify your unhealthy core beliefs:

2. Examine why you would like to let go of these beliefs:

3. Consider the positive and negative consequences of letting go of these beliefs:

4. Brainstorm possible new, healthier core beliefs to replace the old ones:

5. Review History—generate a list of past experiences that combat the old beliefs and support the new ones.

6. Notice old thoughts from your unhealthy beliefs as they arise, and refuse them or refute them.

7. Pay attention to negative behavior patterns and replace them with healthier habits.

8. Solicit feedback from supportive sources.

9. Take a risk—try something that promotes your new belief system.

10. Some remnants of the old system might remain. You'll want to make room for the possibility that growth will occur over time. Show yourself grace, compassion, and acceptance.

Jumpstart the Exercise: Bob's Example

1. Identify your unhealthy core beliefs:

   "I'm inadequate" "I'm not good enough" (from Low Self-Esteem)

2. Examine why you would like to let go of these beliefs:

   I'm tired of feeling bad about myself, I'm tired of comparing myself to other people, and I don't want my poor self-image to hold me back from accomplishing things. Sometimes feeling bad about myself makes me frustrated, and I don't want to become a sad, angry person.

3. Consider the positive and negative consequences of letting go of these beliefs:

   Positive: I might start to feel better about myself, I would be happier, and I wouldn't be afraid to try to achieve something in my life. I would have more confidence, and I wouldn't be so frustrated with myself.

   Negative: My feelings of inadequacy sometimes motivate me to work harder. Those feelings are familiar to me, and it is how I've always thought about myself.

4. Brainstorm possible new, healthier core beliefs to replace the old ones:

   "I'm good exactly as I am."

   "I'm adequate."

   "I'm good enough."

5. Review History—generate a list of past experiences that combat the old beliefs and support the new ones.

   - *In high school, I joined the debate team and won a tournament.*
   - *In college, I studied hard and got my degree.*
   - *In my job, I have a good attendance record and positive relationships with my colleagues.*
   - *My best friend thinks I'm funny.*
   - *I'm a responsible pet-owner.*
   - *I know how to change a tire and change the oil in my car.*

6. Notice old thoughts from your unhealthy beliefs as they arise, and refuse them or refute them.

   - *Last night, my girlfriend mentioned that the air conditioning was making a rattling noise. My first thought was: "I'm not good enough." I assumed that I was a bad partner who let the home fall into disrepair. I told myself that "I'm not good enough" was an outdated and untrue way of thinking. I put that thought away and checked out the noise in the compressor.*
   - *When I went to a staff meeting the other day, I started to avoid participation because of my core belief: "I'm inadequate." I reminded myself that our staff meetings are designed to encourage input from the employees. I told myself, "I'm adequate, and my opinion counts." I then volunteered my perspective on some policy changes.*

7. Pay attention to negative behavior patterns and replace them with healthier habits.

   - *I have a habit of avoiding helping in the kitchen because I assume that my girlfriend won't really want my help because I believe "I'm not adequate." This afternoon, I chopped the tomatoes and prepared a salad instead of assuming I would mess it up. The salad turned out great.*
   - *I tend to torture myself before starting a project at work—telling myself that I don't know what I'm doing,*

that I don't have the skills needed to complete the job, and that everyone sees that I'm not good enough. This time, I started the project and refused to allow myself to indulge in negative thoughts. I tackled the job and spent my time being productive. It felt good.

8. Solicit feedback from supportive sources.

   I told three people about my endeavor to change my core beliefs. I chose people who are dear to me and who always give me support and encouragement.

   - *My girlfriend—she told me that she has always considered me to be more than adequate as a partner. She said that our relationship is a great source of happiness in her life and she wishes that I knew just how wonderful I am.*

   - *My friend Dave—he told me that I'm one of the wittiest people he knows and that I've been a good friend to him for over 15 years. He told me that he thinks my efforts to change my unhealthy core beliefs are impressive and that he's proud of me for being willing to make changes in myself. He said he would help in any way he could.*

   - *My mom – She told me that I had been a delight to her as a child and that she had always been proud of my good grades in school. She told me I've been an excellent son and that I've become like a good friend to her after I became an adult. She said she can't imagine having a kinder, more capable, more intelligent son.*

9. Take a risk—try something that promotes your new belief system.

   I'm joining a rock-climbing group to practice using positive self-talk and to continue working on my confidence level. If I learn how to rock climb, maybe I'll feel proud of myself for trying something new. I want to be brave enough to go ahead and do things that scare me.

10. Some remnants of the old system might remain. You'll want to make room for the possibility that growth will occur over time. Show yourself grace, compassion, and acceptance.

    I'm adequate as I am and don't need to be perfect. Part of the interesting thing about life is being able to accept myself and at the same time be open to growth and change. I'm good enough, and I'm looking forward to learning more about myself, even when I make mistakes.

RULES

Our self-imposed rules grow directly out of our core beliefs. Bob's core belief is, "I'm inadequate." Over time, Bob establishes rules about how he conducts himself. For instance, he might decide—unconsciously—"When I feel inadequate, the rule is that I must restore the balance of power by using intimidation, threats, or force." Following this rule, if Bob sees his girlfriend dancing with someone else, he struts on to the dance floor and threatens to beat up her dance partner.

We create self-destructive rules in order to cope with a distorted core belief system. Then we operate according to these rules without testing their validity or their usefulness. Once you have identified your core beliefs and the rules that are tied to them, the next step is to break those rules! Only by learning to break them can you eliminate old patterns and establish healthier beliefs.

EXERCISE 2: BREAK YOUR DAMAGING RULES

In this exercise you will discover the damaging rules that are tied to your core beliefs, and you will challenge those rules by breaking them. See the *Jumpstart Exercise to help you complete this exercise.*

Evaluate and dismantle your rules by following these steps:

CORE BELIEF 1:

- Damaging "Rule":

- Breaking the Rule:

- Evaluating the Rule:

CORE BELIEF 2:

- Damaging "Rule":

- Breaking the Rule:

- Evaluating the Rule:

CORE BELIEF:

"I will always be rejected."

DAMAGING "RULE":

"When someone rejects my offer for a date, I'll never ask again."

BREAKING THE RULE:

- *First, Dave decides to role-play with a friend—he practices asking someone out on a date.*

- *Second, Dave practices saying hello to a stranger.*

- *Third, Dave compiles a list of possible date candidates.*

- *Fourth, Dave calls or e-mails a couple of those candidates for a casual conversation.*

- *Fifth, Dave pursues those candidates for a low-pressure coffee date.*

- *Sixth, if someone says "No," Dave challenges the rule by reminding himself that the other person could have legitimate reasons for saying no. Dave must be willing to ask again for a different day or time. If the person isn't interested, that doesn't mean Dave is unlovable: He will ask the next person. Dave realizes that his willingness to risk rejection opens him up to more possible dates.*

EVALUATING THE RULE:

Dave sets aside time to assess whether the old rule is valid and healthy or inaccurate and unhealthy. For example, Dave will look at the results of asking out 20 people, and he might discover that more people said "yes" than "no". Even if only one person said "yes", then it still indicates progress.

CORE BELIEF:

"I'm inadequate."

DAMAGING "RULE":

"When I feel inadequate, I will work day and night to compensate for my inadequacy."

BREAKING THE RULE:

- *First, Bob finds a place in his life where he is overcompensating with work.*
- *Second, Bob takes an honest look at how his work schedule is interfering with his overall life balance.*
- *Third, Bob begins to shift some of that work time in small 30-minute increments toward other areas of his life that need attention (more alone time, more time with his girlfriend, etc.)*
- *Fourth, Bob challenges himself to take healthy breaks during work—15 minutes in the morning, a 60-minute lunch, and 15 minutes in the afternoon.*

EVALUATING THE RULE:

Bob compares his old schedule to the new one. Bob asks himself if he feels more balanced, more at peace, healthier. Bob takes time to notice whether the quality of his work has suffered or improved. For example, Bob might discover that he is more rested and that his work performance is higher than before the exercise.

AUTOMATIC THOUGHTS

Bob is at a party when he sees his girlfriend dancing with another guy. The first thought that springs to Bob's mind is, "She's into him." Instantly he assumes, "She's going to get his phone number." Then, he *catastrophizes*, or thinks the worst: "She's going to sleep with him tonight, and I will totally fall apart." This is a classic automatic thought process escalating to an out-of-control level of anger. You no doubt know exactly what that feels like.

It's hard to overestimate how important that first distorted thought is in setting yourself up for rage. The good news is that you can learn to identify and change that reaction. There are actually nine different types of automatic thoughts that can stimulate anger and aggressive behavior.

1. **All-or-Nothing Thinking**: Thinking in terms of absolutes. You might think, *"If I don't make more than $100,000 per year, then I'm worthless."* This kind of thinking leaves you little room to make mistakes, to learn and grow, as we all need to do.

2. **Assumptions**: Thoughts that don't have a factual basis. Bob immediately assumed, *"She's into him."* This is not based on any facts. He doesn't have enough information to give validity to his initial thought.

3. **Catastrophizing**: Jumping straight to the worst-case scenario as if it were inevitable. Bob thinks to himself, *"She's going to sleep with him."* There is nothing to support this theory, but Bob has convinced himself that the situation will turn out to be a catastrophe that he will not be able to withstand.

4. **Shoulds**: Mandating an absolute standard for yourself or someone else. For instance, you might say, *"You should keep the house tidier."* Saying "should" creates stress, decreases positive motivation, and is punitive in nature.

5. **Overgeneralizing**: Making global statements. For instance, *"You always leave your cups around the house,"* or *"You never put your clothes in the hamper."* When you exaggerate a situation by using amplified language (such as "always" and "never"), it creates an environment that is critical and defensive.

6. **Labeling**: Categorizing yourself or someone negatively. If you call someone "dumb," "stupid", "boring," or "lazy," he or she will perceive it as a personal attack, which will lead to an escalation of anger.

7. **Dwelling on the Negative**: Focusing on things that are unproductive or harmful. If you concentrate on one negative aspect of your life—say your disappointment in your son—you'll miss seeing the positives: the wonderful rapport you enjoy with your daughter. Negativity breeds more negativity, which leads to frustration and anger.

8. **Personalizing**: Making yourself more central to a situation than you really are, and not being able to see that other people's responses are not always about you. For instance, if your sister is curt with you on the phone, you might say to yourself, *"She's mad at me."* Her tone may have nothing at all to do with you: She may just have had a bad day at work and is worried she's being laid off.

9. **Blaming**: Viewing other people as being at fault and taking no responsibility for your own role in a problem. For example, if you didn't leave the house on time to get to the movie before it started, you might yell at the cab driver for making you late. In this example, you do not take responsibility for your own role in the problem. You are not willing to admit that you are at fault. You did not get ready early enough to call the cab so that the driver could pick you up with plenty of time to account for traffic.

These automatic thoughts can also result in physical symptoms—increased heart rate, muscle tension, and emotional reactions—like fear, anger, worry, defensiveness and frustration. You are also being very hard on yourself when you succumb to them. Of the many benefits of learning to control your anger, one is that you'll be kinder to yourself.

EXERCISE 3: ANALYZING AUTOMATIC THOUGHTS

This exercise will help you accurately evaluate automatic thoughts that can create aggressive feelings and behaviors. Choose a recent situation where you acted out and then fill out the questions. See the *Jumpstart Exercise to help you complete this exercise.*

1. Date and time of unpleasant situation:

2. Brief description of the situation:

3. Describe your self-talk or automatic thoughts during the situation:

4. Evaluate your automatic thoughts. Do any of those thoughts fit into one of the nine categories?

5. Challenge your automatic thoughts. For each automatic thought, answer the following questions.
   a) What is the evidence that *supports* this thought?

b)   What is the evidence *against* this thought?

c)   Is there another explanation for the situation/event?

d)   What is the worst that could happen? Could I live through it?

e)   What is the best that could happen?

f)   What is the most realistic outcome?

g)   What is the effect of my believing these distorted automatic thoughts?

h)   What could be the positive effect of changing my thinking?

i)   What can I do to make the situation turn out better?

j)   If nothing can be done to improve the situation, how will I cope?

k) What would I tell _____ (a friend) if he or she were facing the same situation?

Jumpstart the Exercise: Megan's Example

1. Date and time of unpleasant situation:

   During Lunch Break on 7/15

2. Brief description of the situation:

   I tried to call my boyfriend, Joe, during lunch break, but he didn't answer. Then, I tried to call a second time 20 minutes later. I started getting really upset.

3. Describe your self-talk or automatic thoughts during the situation:

   "I wonder if he's doing something I wouldn't like?"

   "He must be avoiding me."

   "Is he with another woman?"

4. Evaluate your automatic thoughts. Do any of those thoughts fit into one of the nine categories?

   *I wonder if he's doing something I wouldn't like?"—This thought falls into the category **Dwelling on the Negative**—Because I'm only focusing on the negative possibilities without examining all of the facts.*

   *"He must be avoiding me."— This thought falls into the category **Assumptions**—Because I don't have enough information to be sure that he's avoiding me.*

   *"Is he with another woman?"—This thought falls into the category **Catastrophizing**.—Because I'm leaping to the worst possible conclusion. Then I convince myself that I'm not able to cope with that outcome.*

5. Challenge your automatic thoughts. For each automatic thought, answer the following questions.

   a) What is the evidence that *supports* this thought?

   "I wonder if he's doing something I wouldn't like?"—In the past, men in my life have not returned my calls because they were drinking or doing drugs.

   "He must be avoiding me."—We recently had a fight about my jealousy, and he admitted that he gets sick of me sometimes.

   "Is he with another woman?"—The last man I dated slept with my best friend.

   b) What is the evidence *against* this thought?

   "I wonder if he's doing something I wouldn't like?"—I've never seen him drunk, he has always been honest and responsible, and he works from home with frequent conference calls.

   "He must be avoiding me."—Even after an argument, he never ignores me or holds a grudge, He returns my calls eventually, even when he's busy, and he has always had a legitimate reason when he can't return my calls.

   "Is he with another woman?"—He doesn't go out and party, he doesn't flirt with other women, and he has told me that he is committed to me.

   c) Is there another explanation for the situation/event?

   He's working from home today and is probably on conference calls.

   Something else might have come up because he usually takes my calls— maybe he's visiting a friend and his phone is on "silent," maybe he's on the phone with his boss or a customer, or maybe he's taking a nap.

d) What is the worst that could happen? Could I live through it?

He doesn't want to be with me anymore. I can live with that if I have to, because I've lost people I loved before and I can survive anything short of the loss of food, water, shelter.

e) What is the best that could happen?

He's out shopping for my engagement ring.

f) What is the most realistic outcome?

He'll probably call me later, and he'll have a legitimate explanation for the delayed response.

g) What is the effect of my believing these distorted automatic thoughts?

It creates anxiety. I lose work time. It causes my mind to race with fearful thoughts, Sometimes I have a panic attack. It makes me sad and angry. It causes me to leave him nasty voicemails, and I become accusatory when I do finally talk to him.

h) What could be the positive effect of changing my thinking?

I would feel calmer, I would have more patience, I would be able to let go, I would trust that I could be okay no matter what happened, I could focus on my work, I could explore the situation with Joe in a calm, reasonable manner without anger, and my relationship could improve.

i) What can I do to make the situation turn out better?

I could take a break at work and go walk the stairs, I could call a friend for a reality check, I could look at the situation from different perspectives, I could challenge my distorted automatic thoughts, and I could focus on work tasks.

j) If nothing can be done to improve the situation, how will I cope?

I can spend more time with friends and family, I can go to a counselor, I can go work out, I can practice deep breathing exercises, I can try to understand Joe's side of the situation, I can evaluate my boundaries, needs, and expectations, and I can explore the pros and cons of staying in the relationship.

k) What would I tell _____ (a friend) if he or she were facing the same situation?

I would tell my friend Sarah that fear is clouding her judgment. I would explain that her boyfriend has always been reliable and honest. I would encourage her to take a time-out to evaluate her thoughts. I would reassure her that she is loved by many people, no matter what happens with her boyfriend.

HALTING HARMFUL HABITS

I've noticed that people who reported high levels of anger had the most trouble with All-or-Nothing Thinking, Assumptions, and Catastrophizing. In the following exercises, you will focus on these automatic thoughts. Once you HALT these three habitual ways of thinking, you will feel emotionally healthier, less at the mercy of unmanageable thoughts, and more in control of your anger.

ALL-OR-NOTHING THINKING

All-or-Nothing Thinking, one of the nine distorted automatic thoughts, is absolute, rigid, and centered on perfectionism. Remember the earlier example of All-or-Nothing Thinking: *"If I don't make more than $100,000 per year, then I'm worthless."* When you think in terms of absolutes, you leave yourself little room to make mistakes, to celebrate accomplishments, and to learn and grow.

All-or-Nothing Thinking creates a fear of failure. When you are motivated by a fear of failure, you are never satisfied with achievements and you are overly critical of performance. The intensity of criticism, inflexibility, and fear leads to frustration and anger, often directed outwardly.

EXERCISE 4: HALT ALL-OR-NOTHING THINKING

The purpose of this exercise is to help spring you from the All-or-Nothing trap. See the ***Jumpstart Exercise to help you complete this exercise.***

1. Examine the Thought

    a) Describe a situation where you experienced All-or-Nothing Thinking:

    b) What were your thoughts?

    c) How did you feel?

    d) How did you act?

2. Challenge and Reframe the Thought

    a) What is the evidence that *supports* this thought?

    b) What is the evidence *against* this thought?

    c) Is there another explanation for the situation/event?

    d) What is the worst that could happen? Could I live through it?

    e) What is the best that could happen?

    f) What is the most realistic outcome?

    g) What is the effect of my believing these All-or-Nothing Thoughts?

h) What could be the positive effect of changing my thinking?

i) What can I do to make the situation turn out better?

j) If nothing can be done to improve the situation, how will I cope?

k) What would I tell _____ (a friend) if he or she were facing the same situation?

HALT THE THOUGHT

1. Celebrate small accomplishments. Focus on positive outcomes by looking at all of the variables in a situation. Notice even minor accomplishments.

   a) Within the situation that you describe above, were there minor accomplishments that you failed to notice because of All-or-Nothing Thinking?

      Circle: Yes or No

   b) What were the minor accomplishments that you minimized or failed to notice in that situation?

2. Look for gray. Realize that things are almost never black and white. People, situations, and environments are very different and multilayered. When you are viewing a situation, it is important to make room for complexity because not all people, situations, and environments are clearly defined or easily categorized.

a) Within the situation that you describe above, were there areas of gray that you ignored or oversimplified because of All-or-Nothing Thinking?

Circle: Yes or No

b) What were those areas of gray that you ignored or oversimplified in that situation?

3. Relax. All-or-Nothing Thinking creates tension and stress. When you are operating out of fear, it helps to take a break and relax in order to gain perspective.

a) Within the situation you described, did you feel your tension increasing as you engaged in All-or-Nothing Thinking?

Circle: Yes or No

b) How did you know you were feeling tension and stress? What did you experience?

c) Next time a situation like this arises, pay attention to your breathing, muscle tension, perspiration, temperature, and heart rate. Take time to do something that relaxes you, and then return to your thoughts about the situation with a new outlook.

4. Become less critical. Try not to categorize people or events into "Good versus Bad" or "Right versus Wrong." All-or-Nothing Thinking can cause individuals to unfairly label people or situations.

a) Within the situation described above, did you find yourself categorizing or criticizing?

Circle: Yes or No

b) Challenge yourself to be more understanding and less judgmental. Be more accepting of differences. What were the criticisms you made earlier, and how might you change your thoughts so that they could be less critical?

5. Manage expectations. When you have unrealistically high expectations of yourself and others, you will tend to judge harshly. All-or-Nothing Thinking creates unrealistic expectations and leads to disappointment.

    a) Within the situation described above, did you have unrealistic expectations?

        Circle: Yes or No

    b) What is a more realistic expectation?

6. Remain Flexible. When you're rigid and inflexible, it is more difficult to solve problems, generate ideas, maintain relationships, and deal with conflict. All-or-Nothing Thinking comes from a rigid mind-set, which creates frustration, anger, and anxiety.

    a) Within the situation described above, were you being rigid or inflexible?

        Circle: Yes or No

    b) How could you change your thinking so that it would be more open and flexible?

Jumpstart the Exercise: Bob's Example

1. Examine the Thought

   a) Describe a situation where you experienced All-or-Nothing Thinking:

   I remember when I got a paycut at work—I got extremely upset.

   b) What were your thoughts?

   I thought, "If I don't show that I can provide financial stability, then my girlfriend will never marry me."

   c) How did you feel?

   I felt ashamed and inadequate, fearful.

   d) How did you act?

   I became furious and defensive, stormed around the house ranting about the injustice of it all.

2. Challenge and Reframe the Thought

   a) What is the evidence that *supports* this thought?

   In my family, my father was the provider, and my mom valued his ability to take care of finances.

   b) What is the evidence *against* this thought?

   There are people who fall in love with other people who aren't financially successful. My girlfriend says she doesn't care about having lots of "things."

   c) Is there another explanation for the situation/event?

   There was a downturn at my company, and it's probably temporary. Things will improve, I hope.

   d) What is the worst that could happen? Could I live through it?

   Worst-Case Scenario: I could end up without a job. Yes, I could live through that. Other people do it all the time. Or my girlfriend could leave me for a man who has a better job. I could live through that, but I hope that won't happen.

   e) What is the best that could happen?

   My boss could reward my patience by giving me a promotion when things improve. . . . my girlfriend would be impressed and proud, and I could afford to get her an engagement ring.

   f) What is the most realistic outcome?

   I'll tighten my budget for awhile, and then things will get better. My girlfriend will help me make a budget for us to live on for a while.

   g) What is the effect of my believing these All-or-Nothing Thoughts?

   Getting riled up and believing that I have to be a great professional success all the time makes me feel stressed out and inadequate. It puts pressure on me and on my partner.

   h) What could be the positive effect of changing my thinking?

   I would be easier to live with, and I would be a calmer employee. I might be a better leader if I didn't fly off the handle so much.

i) What can I do to make the situation turn out better?

I could sit down and think things through before overreacting. I could remember my worth as a person, not just as a provider. I could trust my girlfriend to love me for who I am, not what I have.

j) If nothing can be done to improve the situation, how will I cope?

I will remind myself that I'm strong enough to handle any setbacks in work that come my way. I'll take a walk, use deep breathing, and try to have more balance in my thoughts.

k) What would I tell _____ (a friend) if he or she were facing the same situation?

I would tell Dave that his job is only one part of who he is, that he can recognize when he's doing All-or-Nothing Thinking and remember that it's not helpful to think that way. I would tell him to remember his strength and his value as a person and not to place a number on it.

HALT THE THOUGHT

1. Celebrate small accomplishments. Focus on positive outcomes by looking at all of the variables in a situation. Notice even minor accomplishments.

    a) Within the situation that you describe above, were there minor accomplishments that you failed to notice because of All-or-Nothing Thinking?

    Circle: **Yes** or No

    b) What were the minor accomplishments that you minimized or failed to notice in that situation?

    Well, I do HAVE a job at all. I also have a girlfriend who loves me. It's not all about my paycheck.

2. Look for gray. Realize that things are almost never black and white. People, situations, and environments are very different and multilayered. When you are viewing a situation, it is important to make room for complexity because not all people, situations, and environments are clearly defined or easily categorized.

    a) Within the situation that you describe above, were there areas of gray that you ignored or oversimplified because of All-or-Nothing Thinking?

    Circle: **Yes** or No

    b) What were those areas of gray that you ignored or oversimplified in that situation?

    It's as if I have a magic number in my head and if I don't match that number, then I'm inadequate and unlovable. I ignored the gray area of the fact that I do make a living, but it's simply not as much as I would like to make. I also oversimplified my girlfriend, thinking she was grading me on a "Pass/Fail" basis. She actually has more kindness, more compassion, and more depth than that.

3. Relax. All-or-Nothing Thinking creates tension and stress. When you are operating out of fear, it helps to take a break and relax in order to gain perspective.

    a) Within the situation you described, did you feel your tension increasing as you engaged in All-or-Nothing Thinking?

    Circle: **Yes** or No

    b) How did you know you were feeling tension and stress? What did you experience?

    I felt my heart beat faster. I started pacing, and I felt like I was breathing fast.

    c) Next time a situation like this arises, pay attention to your breathing, muscle tension, perspiration, temperature, and heart rate. Take time to do something that relaxes you, and then return to your thoughts about the situation with a new outlook.

4. Become less critical. Try not to categorize people or events into "Good versus Bad" or "Right versus Wrong." All-or-Nothing Thinking can cause us to unfairly label people or situations.

    a) Within the situation described above, did you find yourself categorizing or criticizing?

    Circle: **Yes** or No

    b) Challenge yourself to be more understanding and less judgmental. Be more accepting of differences. What were the criticisms you made earlier, and how might you change your thoughts so that they could be less critical?

    I told myself I was "bad" or "inadequate" because of my pay decrease. I judged myself harshly. I also judged my girlfriend as intolerant of financial difficulty, which wasn't fair. I need to remember who I really am and who my girlfriend really is, so that I won't jump into All-or-Nothing Thinking.

5. Manage expectations—When you have unrealistically high expectations of yourself and others, you will tend to judge harshly. All-or-Nothing Thinking creates unrealistic expectations and leads to disappointment.

    a) Within the situation described above, did you have unrealistic expectations?

    Circle: **Yes** or No

    b) What is a more realistic expectation?

    I expected not to face a financial setback. I thought I would just work hard and move steadily forward. It's more realistic to expect to face problems, even when I'm making progress.

6. Remain Flexible. When you're rigid and inflexible, it is more difficult to solve problems, generate ideas, maintain relationships, and deal with conflict. All-or-Nothing Thinking comes from a rigid mind-set, which creates frustration, anger, and anxiety.

    a) Within the situation described above, were you being rigid or inflexible?

    Circle: **Yes** or No

    b) How could you change your thinking so that it would be more open and flexible?

    Not sticking to my idea that money equals worth. Understanding that love does not have to be conditional. I would change my thinking to include all of the other valuable things about myself. I would try to roll with things better. I might have considered the setback as an opportunity to show greater team¬work with my girlfriend.

ASSUMING

Assuming is guessing without having all the facts. Remember the earlier example of Bob's automatic assumption, *"She's into him"*? This is not a factually based thought because he does not have enough information to validate it.

When you make an assumption without all the facts, it leads to an escalation of anger, overreaction, and an inaccurate behavioral response. Assuming is an enemy of healthy communication and conflict resolution.

EXERCISE 5: HALT ASSUMING

The purpose of this exercise is help you examine, reframe, and HALT Assuming. See the ***Jumpstart Exercise to help you complete this exercise.***

1. Examine the Thought

   a) Describe a situation below where you made assumptions:

   b) What were your thoughts?

   c) How did you feel?

   d) How did you act?

2. Challenge and Reframe the Thought

   a) What is the evidence that *supports* this thought?

b) What is the evidence *against* this thought?

c) Is there another explanation for the situation/event?

d) What is the worst that could happen? Could I live through it?

e) What is the best that could happen?

f) What is the most realistic outcome?

g) What is the effect of my believing these assumptions?

h) What could be the positive effect of changing my thinking?

i) What can I do to make the situation turn out better?

j)   If nothing can be done to improve the situation, how will I cope?

k)   What would I tell _____ (a friend) if he or she were facing the same situation?

HALT THE THOUGHT

1. Focus on the facts and behaviors that can be measured. Take time to evaluate all the facts within a situation before you make conclusions. Observe the behaviors of others in order to define clearly what is happening in the moment.

   a) Within the situation that you describe above, did you make assumptions?

   Circle: Yes or No

   b) Write out all the facts about the situation:

   c) What behaviors can be measured? Clearly describe the behaviors themselves.

2. Ask questions and communicate. Gather more information before coming up with a theory. Be willing to ask yourself and others for extra data before leaping to conclusions about motives, agendas, and meaning.

   a) Within the situation that you describe above, were there more questions you could have asked to gain a more accurate perspective?

   Circle: Yes or No

   b) What were some of the questions that you could have asked in order to gather more information?

3. Determine if your assumptions could be false or incorrect. Do not always think that your perspective is 100 percent accurate. In fact, it is safe to imagine that your first assumption might be incorrect.

   a) Within the situation that you describe above, did you go with your first assumption?

   Circle: Yes or No

   b) Was that assumption useful or was it harmful to resolving the situation? How so?

c) How did holding on to your assumption lead you toward an incorrect conclusion?

4. Value differences of opinion. Approach disagreement with respect and curiosity. Maintain an open mind and be willing to consider other perspectives.

   a) Within the situation that you describe above, did you value other perspectives?

   Circle: Yes or No

   b) What differences of opinion did you find hard to accept?

   c) What differences will you need to try to embrace in order to make room for a broader set of ideas, thoughts, and opinions?

Jumpstart the Exercise: Bob's Example

1. Examine the Thought

    a) Describe a situation below where you made assumptions:

    I assumed that my girlfriend was "into him" (the guy she was dancing with). It led to other, worse thoughts.

    b) What were your thoughts?

    I thought, "She's into him," "I'm not good enough for her," "Why would she do this to me?" "She's rude and disrespectful!"

    c) How did you feel?

    I felt jealous, fearful, betrayed, angry.

    d) How did you act?

    I behaved furiously— I stomped onto the dance floor and threatened to beat up the other guy.

2. Challenge and Reframe the Thought

    a) What is the evidence that *supports* this thought?

    Well, I could see her dancing with someone else with my own two eyes.

    b) What is the evidence *against* this thought?

    I don't actually know her thoughts. I can't read her mind, so I can't be sure my girlfriend is into this other guy.

    c) Is there another explanation for the situation/event?

    Maybe she was caught off guard and was just being nice. Maybe she was wishing I would ask her to dance. Anyway, later I found out the guy was her cousin.

    d) What is the worst that could happen? Could I live through it?

    Worst—That she was infatuated with that other guy and was already planning to leave me for him. Yes, I could live through it, but I would be extremely unhappy.

    e) What is the best that could happen?

    I could find out that the whole thing meant nothing to her at all—that the guy (in fact!) was her cousin.

    f) What is the most realistic outcome?

    Well, now I know what really was going on, and so I know the answer … but the most probable outcome was simply that my girlfriend was dancing with someone else and that it was just a dance, nothing more.

    g) What is the effect of my believing these assumptions?

    I overreacted and threatened the guy.

    h) What could be the positive effect of changing my thinking?

    I would feel more relaxed and in control, better able to see all possibilities instead of focusing on one terrible thought.

    i) What can I do to make the situation turn out better?

    I'm sure it would have turned out better no matter what, if I had not acted out in such a shocking way. I could have gathered more facts before jumping to conclusions.

j) If nothing can be done to improve the situation, how will I cope?

If it had been the worst-case scenario, I would have had to have an adult conversation with my girl-friend to gather information about the situation and our relationship. Then, I would have found support from my friends to get through the grief if the relationship ended.

k) What would I tell _____ (a friend) if he or she were facing the same situation?

I would tell Dave to calm down and take a deep breath before freaking out. I would tell him not to jump to conclusions or make immediate assumptions. I would tell him to get information and be thoughtful about his actions.

HALT THE THOUGHT

1. Focus on the facts and behaviors that can be measured. Take time to evaluate all the facts within a situation before you make conclusions. Observe the behaviors of others in order to define clearly what is happening in the moment.

    a) Within the situation that you describe above, did you make assumptions?

    Circle: **Yes** or No

    b) Write out all the facts about the situation:

    - *My girlfriend says she loves me and wants to marry me some day.*
    - *My girlfriend was dancing with someone else.*
    - *I didn't know that guy.*
    - *We were at a public event.*

    c) What behaviors can be measured? Clearly describe the behaviors themselves.

    - *My girlfriend was just dancing, not nuzzling or kissing the other guy.*
    - *There was no other information to measure.*

2. Ask questions and communicate. Gather more information before coming up with a theory. Be willing to ask yourself and others for extra data before leaping to conclusions about motives, agendas, and meaning.

    a) Within the situation that you describe above, were there more questions you could have asked to gain a more accurate perspective?

    Circle: **Yes** or No

    b) What were some of the questions that you could have asked in order to gather more information?

    At some point, I could have asked my girlfriend, "Who was that guy you were dancing with?" and if I still felt bothered, I could ask her, "Are you still happy being with me?"

3. Determine if your assumptions could be false or incorrect. Do not always think that your perspective is 100 percent accurate. In fact, it is safe to imagine that your first assumption might be incorrect.

    a) Within the situation that you describe above, did you go with your first assumption?

    Circle: **Yes** or No

b) Was that assumption useful, or was it harmful to resolving the situation? How so?

- *I immediately assumed, "She's into him."— It was not useful, it was wrong, and it was harmful.*

- *The thought prompted me to overreact, the guy was her cousin, and I behaved terribly.*

c) How did holding on to your assumption lead you toward an incorrect conclusion?

I held on to my assumption until I knew it was her cousin, but by then it was too late. I had acted like a jerk. The assumption sent me into an upward spiral of rage and fear. I concluded that she would end up sleeping with that guy, which seems ridiculous to me now.

4. Value differences of opinion. Approach disagreement with respect and curiosity. Maintain an open mind and be willing to consider other perspectives.

a) Within the situation that you describe above, did you value other perspectives?

Circle: Yes or **No**

b) What differences of opinion did you find hard to accept?

I couldn't make room for any other information beyond my first assumption.

c) What differences will you need to try to embrace in order to make room for a broader set of ideas, thoughts, and opinions?

I need to remember that other people aren't always out to hurt me. I need to embrace the love and trust my girlfriend offers me. I need to remember that threats and intimidation are not constructive.

CATASTROPHIZING

Catastrophizing means expecting the worst outcome. It's based in fear and anxiety. Remember Bob's example of catastrophizing, "She's going to sleep with him." Bob had convinced himself that the situation would become a catastrophe and that he would not be able to cope with it.

Operating in a fear mentality can lead to a sense of urgency and aggression that can cause you to react rashly rather than respond intelligently.

See the Jumpstart Exercise to help you complete this exercise.

EXERCISE 6: HALT CATASTROPHIZING

1. Examine the Thought

    a) Describe a situation in which you were catastrophizing:

    b) What were your thoughts?

    c) How did you feel?

    d) How did you act?

2. Challenge and Reframe the Thought

    a) What is the evidence that *supports* this thought?

b) What is the evidence *against* this thought?

c) Is there another explanation for the situation/event?

d) What is the worst that could happen? Could I live through it?

e) What is the best that could happen?

f) What is the most realistic outcome?

g) What is the effect of my believing these catastrophizing thoughts?

h) What could be the positive effect of changing my thinking?

i) What can I do to make the situation turn out better?

j)   If nothing can be done to improve the situation, how will I cope?

k)   What would I tell _____(a friend) if he or she were facing the same situation?

HALT THE THOUGHT

1. Look at all of the plausible outcomes beyond the worst-case scenario. There are many possible outcomes within any given situation. Take time to explore all of the possible outcomes and narrow it down to the most realistic possibility.

   a) Within the situation that you describe above did you focus on one worst-case scenario?

   Circle: Yes or No

   b) Describe the worst-case prediction below:

   c) Describe other possible outcomes below:

   Outcome 1:

   Outcome 2:

   Outcome 3:

   Go over the above list, including your original possibility, and narrow it down to the most realistic outcome. Make sure you evaluate the three possibilities based on reality and not fear.

2. Learn to cope. Catastrophizing is about trying to control situations and outcomes through anxious thinking. This unhealthy control strategy is usually an attempt to deal with uncertainty. Becoming comfortable with being uncomfortable is vital in dealing with uncertainty.

   a) Within the situation that you described above, did you try to cope with uncertainty by using catastrophizing thoughts?

   Circle: Yes or No

   b) How did catastrophizing help you cope with the situation?

   c) What are other ways to cope with uncertain outcomes? Example: deep breathing, progressive muscle relaxation, physical exercise, examine your thoughts, understand that discomfort doesn't equal disaster, and so on.

3. Get busy and gain control. Even if the worst outcome is the most probable outcome, there are still measures you can take to be proactive and gain as much control over the situation as possible. Being practical and getting down to business will help you feel less anxious and therefore better able to deal with anger, frustration, and conflict.

    a) Within the situation that you describe above did you find that you felt paralyzed, overwhelmed, or excessively anxious because of catastrophizing?

        Circle: Yes or No

    b) What steps could you have taken to prevent or mitigate an unpleasant outcome?

    c) What could you have done to feel more competent and capable, despite potential discomfort, setbacks, or problems? (Remember: Don't react—instead, respond intelligently. Come up with a reasonable plan.)

    d) What areas did you have control over, and what areas do you need to relinquish control?

    e) How will you cope the next time this problem presents itself?

Jumpstart the Exercise: Bob's Example

1. Examine the Thought

    a) Describe a situation in which you were catastrophizing:

    *When I saw my girlfriend dancing with another guy, I made assumptions and then catastrophically concluded, "**She's going to sleep with him**."*

    b) What were your thoughts?

    - *"I can't believe this is happening"*
    - *"Who does he think he is?"*
    - *"I'm not going to let myself be pushed around like this!"*
    - *"What is she thinking?"*

    c) How did you feel?

    I felt jealous, fearful, betrayed, embarrassed, angry.

    d) How did you act?

    I freaked out. I threatened the guy.

2. Challenge and Reframe the Thought

    a) What is the evidence that *supports* this thought?

    She was dancing with him, but that's all.

    b) What is the evidence *against* this thought?

    My girlfriend has always been faithful, and she tells me she wants to be with me forever.

    c) Is there another explanation for the situation/event?

    Well, it turns out he was her cousin. But even if that had not been the case, I guess it would have been reasonable for her to want to dance with someone other than me that night. She's a fun girl who makes lots of friends.

    d) What is the worst that could happen? Could I live through it?

    She could have had sex with him that night. Yes, it would be very, very hard, but I could live through it.

    e) What is the best that could happen?

    I would wake up and it would have all been a bad dream.

    f) What is the most realistic outcome?

    That it was no big deal. She just danced with someone else.

    g) What is the effect of my believing these catastrophizing thoughts?

    I got overly fearful and upset. I flew into a rage. I couldn't see anything positive.

    h) What could be the positive effect of changing my thinking?

    I would be able to recognize catastrophizing thoughts as they happened and I would be able to talk myself out of them.

i) What can I do to make the situation turn out better?

I can wait to get the true facts, I can be more open to outside information, and I can be more reasonable and balanced in the way I evaluate a situation. I can ask for help before I do something unwise.

j) If nothing can be done to improve the situation, how will I cope?

I will call my mom or my friend Dave. I will ask for support. I will focus on the good parts of my life.

k) What would I tell _____(a friend) if he or she were facing the same situation?

I would tell Dave to relax and think before he reacts. I would tell him not to magnify or exaggerate his negative perceptions. I would tell him this thing that I heard a lady say once. She said, "Your feelings are real, but they are not reality."

HALT THE THOUGHT

1. Look at all of the plausible outcomes beyond the worst case scenario. There are many possible outcomes within any given situation. Take time to explore all of the possible outcomes and narrow it down to the most realistic possibility.

   a) Within the situation that you describe above did you focus on one worst case scenario?

      Circle: **Yes** or No

   b) Describe the worst-case prediction below:

      My girlfriend would sleep with the guy she was dancing with.

   c) Describe other possible outcomes below:

      Outcome 1: My girlfriend was harmlessly flirting with another guy but didn't intend to take it very far.

      Outcome 2: Maybe I had understood it all wrong—maybe the guy on the dance floor was her good friend from the past, or her uncle or cousin, or someone who was not a threat to me at all.

      Outcome 3: My girlfriend wanted to dance with someone who knew how to salsa instead of dancing with me, when she knows I'm not a great dancer. Maybe she thought I needed a break from dancing.

      Go over the above list, including your original possibility, and narrow it down to the most realistic outcome. Make sure you evaluate the three possibilities based on reality and not fear.

2. Learn to cope. Catastrophizing is about trying to control situations and outcomes through anxious thinking. This unhealthy control strategy is usually an attempt to deal with uncertainty. Becoming comfortable with being uncomfortable is vital in dealing with uncertainty.

   a) Within the situation that you described above, did you try to cope with uncertainty by using catastrophizing thoughts?

      Circle: **Yes** or No

   b) How did catastrophizing help you cope with the situation?

      It didn't, although I guess I felt more powerful when I was enraged than when I felt fearful.

   c) What are other ways to cope with uncertain outcomes? Example: deep breathing, progressive muscle relaxation, physical exercise, examine your thoughts, understand that discomfort doesn't equal disaster, and so on. (We will discuss these techniques in subsequent chapters.)

I could have gone for a walk or waited to talk to my girlfriend. I could have taken a deep breath and counted to 10.

3. Get busy and gain control. Even if the worst outcome is the most probable outcome, there are still measures you can take to be proactive and gain as much control over the situation as possible. Being practical and getting down to business will help you feel less anxious and therefore better able to deal with anger, frustration, and conflict.

a) Within the situation that you describe above did you find that you felt paralyzed, overwhelmed, or excessively anxious because of catastrophizing?

Circle: **Yes** or No

b) What steps could you have taken to prevent or mitigate an unpleasant outcome?

I could have spent time formulating my thoughts—reminding myself not to exaggerate or magnify what I see in front of me. I could have waited to ask questions until later, when we were alone and I was feeling calmer.

c) What could you have done to feel more competent and capable, despite potential discomfort, setbacks, or problems? (Remember: Don't react—instead, respond intelligently. Come up with a reasonable plan.)

I could have reviewed the success of my relationship and asked myself to be more realistic in the way I evaluated my girlfriend's behavior.

d) What areas did you have control over, and what areas do you need to relinquish control?

I can control my own reactions, but I should not try to control my girlfriend and who she dances with.

e) How will you cope the next time this problem presents itself?

I will slow down, challenge my catastrophizing thoughts, and wait until an appropriate time to investigate.

CHAPTER TWO

Your Anger Cycles and Triggers

Okay, so by now I hope you have a pretty good grasp of the beliefs and rules that have been driving your anger to dangerous peaks. When we're struggling with anger, we tend to escalate or "ascend vertically" as we react to upsetting events. Each reaction leads to another, creating an intensifying cycle that ends in an explosion. The accompanying chart shows how Bob's anger cycle brought him from 0 to 10 in the blink of an eye. Read from the bottom up and you can see clearly how this happened.

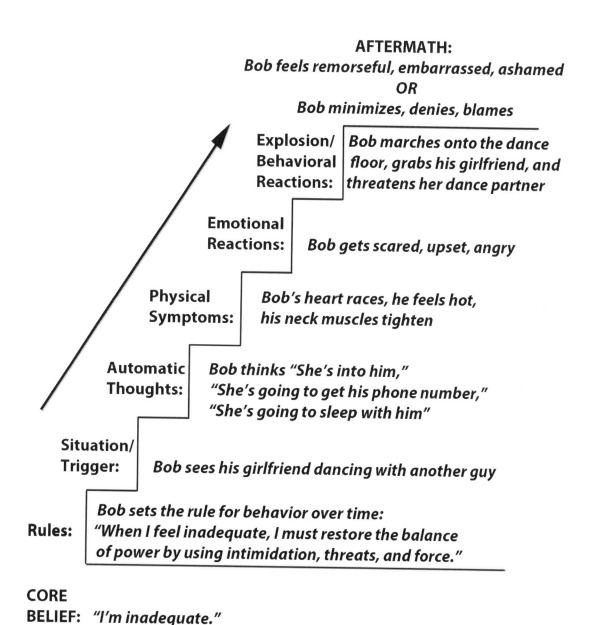

AFTERMATH:
Bob feels remorseful, embarrassed, ashamed
OR
Bob minimizes, denies, blames

Explosion/ Behavioral Reactions: *Bob marches onto the dance floor, grabs his girlfriend, and threatens her dance partner*

Emotional Reactions: *Bob gets scared, upset, angry*

Physical Symptoms: *Bob's heart races, he feels hot, his neck muscles tighten*

Automatic Thoughts: *Bob thinks "She's into him," "She's going to get his phone number," "She's going to sleep with him"*

Situation/ Trigger: *Bob sees his girlfriend dancing with another guy*

Rules: *Bob sets the rule for behavior over time: "When I feel inadequate, I must restore the balance of power by using intimidation, threats, and force."*

CORE BELIEF: *"I'm inadequate."*

EXERCISE 7: YOUR ANGER CYCLE

Think back to the last time your anger went from 0 to 10 before you could do anything to halt it. Try to remember exactly what happened—your triggers, thoughts, feelings, physical symptoms, and responses. Now chart your own vertical ascent on the following diagram.

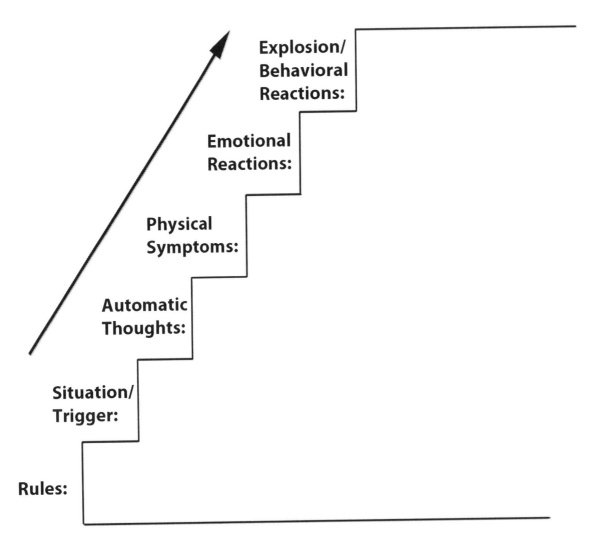

AFTERMATH:

Explosion/
Behavioral
Reactions:

Emotional
Reactions:

Physical
Symptoms:

Automatic
Thoughts:

Situation/
Trigger:

Rules:

CORE
BELIEF:

ANGER TRIGGERS

A client of mine, Martin, was living with a woman named Liz who had a big problem with his former girlfriends. One day Liz was cleaning out a closet and found a scarf stuffed way in the back that an old girlfriend had given Martin. Liz was so insecure that any sign he had ever been involved with anyone else set her off for hours. Well, Liz had four hours to ruminate on the significance of a crummy gift before Martin came home. She jumped all over him, screaming and yelling, asking him why he would keep the scarf, accusing him of holding on to the former lover, and being unfaithful. Liz had been triggered because her past relationships had been filled with cheating. It didn't matter to her what she knew to be true: She *felt* as if Martin had cheated. Eventually, if she doesn't get a grip on her triggers, she's going to drive him out of her life into someone else's arms for real.

If you keep on doing what you've always done, you will keep getting the same results. It's what I call the "Oh, no, here we go again…" syndrome. When you hear that in your own mind, it's a big flashing neon sign that your anger is escalating. It's time to take your hand off the trigger!

EXERCISE 8: ANGER TRIGGERS

When you recognize a recurrent thought, subject/topic, place, body sensation, or behavior, you can predict what always comes next. Then you can slow down and shift your attitude and behavior to "take your hand off the trigger." See the *Jumpstart Exercise to help you complete this exercise.*

Answer the questions below to get to know your own triggers:

THOUGHTS

1. What kinds of thoughts stimulate your anger?

2. Do you tend to dwell on the negative?

3. Do you catastrophize, or assume the worst will happen?

4. Do you make assumptions about people/places/situations?

5. Do you make "should" statements?

6. How do your thoughts change as you become angry?

7. Do your thoughts race?

8. Do you ruminate or stew?

9. Does your thinking become cloudy?

10. Does your mind go blank when you get angry?

11. What kinds of thoughts do you have after an anger episode?

12. Do you have thoughts of blame?

13. Do you justify your actions?

14. Do you minimize your actions?

15. Do you deny your role in the conflict?

FEELINGS

16. What kinds of feelings stimulate your anger?

17. Do you become angry when you feel hurt or disappointed?

18. Do you become angry when you feel disrespected?

19. Do you become angry when you feel fearful or anxious?

20. Do you become angry when you feel surprised or caught off guard?

21. Do you become angry when you feel embarrassed?

22. How do your feelings change as you become angry?

23. Do your feelings intensify?

24. Do you feel flooded or overwhelmed?

25. Do your feelings shut down or turn off?

26. What kinds of feelings do you have after an anger episode?

27. Do you feel ashamed or guilty?

28. Do you feel embarrassed?

29. Do you feel resentful?

30. Do you feel justified or vindicated?

SUBJECTS/TOPICS

31. What kinds of subjects stimulate your anger?

32. Do you tend to get into arguments about money?

33. Do you tend to get into arguments about religion?

34. Do you tend to get into arguments about politics?

35. Do you tend to get into arguments about work?

36. Do you tend to get into arguments about family?

37. Do you tend to get into arguments about time?

PLACES

38. Are there certain places where you find yourself getting angry more often?

39. Where do you tend to have arguments? (Bedroom, living room, kitchen, yard, dining room, your in-law's house, etc.?)

40. Do you tend to get angry in your car?

41. Do you tend to get angry at your place of employment?

42. Do you tend to get angry while standing in queue?

BODY SENSATIONS

43. What physical sensations do you tend to notice when you become angry?

44. Do you experience changes in body temperature, heart rate, muscle tension, digestion, respiration rate, salivation, perspiration, and/or diameter of the pupils?

45. Do you experience headaches, stomachaches, back or neck pain?

BEHAVIORS

46. What behaviors do you exhibit as you become angry?

47. Do you "time travel"— meaning do you hold on to grudges, bring up the past, and/or review old offenses?

48. Do you slam doors, throw things, hit the wall, curse, scream, name-call, threaten, blame, sulk, or stew?

49. Do you hit, grab, punch, shove, push, kick, spit, pinch, or bite?

50. Do you threaten others with weapons?

51. Do you threaten suicide or homicide?

Jumpstart the Exercise: Bob's Example

THOUGHTS

1. What kinds of thoughts stimulate your anger?

   - *Thoughts like "Why don't people listen to me?"*
   - *"How do I always end up being ignored?"*
   - *"No one really thinks I'm worth anything."*

2. Do you tend to dwell on the negative?

   Constantly. It's hard for me to stay positive when I just don't expect positive things to happen. They usually don't.

3. Do you catastrophize or assume the worst outcome?

   Yes, especially when it comes to my girlfriend. I always think she's going to leave me for someone else.

4. Do you make assumptions about people/places/situations?

   Yes, I assume that I'll be judged, that people won't like me, that I'll have to work harder than other people just to be normal, that I'll never succeed, and that the world is against me.

5. Do you make "should" statements?

   Yes, often I think that my girlfriend "should" pay more attention to me. Then again, I spend a lot of time thinking about how I "should" be different, better, and smarter.

6. How do your thoughts change as you become angry?

   My thoughts come faster and take over my head—everything else shrinks away.

7. Do your thoughts race?

   Yes, it's almost like the thoughts tumble out one after the other.

8. Do you ruminate or stew?

   When I'm alone, yes, I do. I think about all of the ways I've been done wrong, and I think about all of the things I wish I could change.

9. Does your thinking become cloudy?

   Not really—I usually feel like things become crystal clear when I'm mad.

10. Does your mind go blank when you are angry?

    Only if I'm at the peak of my rage—when it seems like nothing can ever make things right.

11. What kinds of thoughts do you have after an anger episode?

    When I'm really, really mad, I think about how irritating the other person is, how much he or she has done wrong, and how I can't trust that person.

12. Do you have thoughts of blame?

    Yes. Other people just don't treat me right. It happens all the time.

13. Do you justify your actions?

Yes, I guess I do. Even when I do something unforgiveable, I can usually think of a reason to explain why it was understandable for me to act that way.

14. Do you minimize your actions?

After a fight, I usually try to get my girlfriend to see that what I did really wasn't so bad after all—that it was minor compared to what other guys do to their girlfriends.

15. Do you deny your role in the conflict?

Sometimes. . . well, maybe a lot. Sometimes I feel like none of it was my fault and that I did nothing wrong—that the other person is completely responsible and I'm an innocent victim. I guess that's not very realistic.

FEELINGS

16. What kinds of feelings stimulate your anger?

Jealousy, frustration, impatience.

17. Do you become angry when you feel hurt or disappointed?

Yes.

18. Do you become angry when you feel disrespected?

Absolutely.

19. Do you become angry when you feel fearful or anxious?

I guess so . . . I never thought about that before, but yes, I do.

20. Do you become angry when you feel surprised or caught off guard?

For at least a moment, yes, until I regain control.

21. Do you become angry when you feel embarrassed?

Yes, because it's humiliating for people to see me do something stupid, and I don't think it's right for other people to laugh at me or make jokes at my expense.

22. How do your feelings change as you become angry?

They become bigger and take over.

23. Do your feelings intensify?

Yes, very much.

24. Do you feel flooded or overwhelmed? (When someone feels "flooded," that person typically feels like there are too many words or feelings or experiences happening at once. It becomes difficult to process all of the emotional information, so the person simply shuts down.)

Sometimes I get flooded—and I either go numb or I have to "do something."

25. Do your feelings shut down or turn off?

Yes, that happens sometimes.

26. What kinds of feelings do you have after an anger episode?

   I feel resentful about being pushed to the point of anger, I feel justified in my reaction, and I obsess about how wrong the other person was.

27. Do you feel ashamed or guilty?

   I guess I do sometimes.

28. Do you feel embarrassed?

   When I do something dumb in a moment of anger, yes, I feel embarrassed afterward.

29. Do you feel resentful?

   All the time.

30. Do you feel justified or vindicated?

   Yes, especially if I'm able to make my point forcefully so that the other person sees how wrong he or she was.

SUBJECTS/TOPICS

31. What kinds of subjects stimulate your anger?

   Cheating, politics, criticism, my career or financial situation.

32. Do you tend to get into arguments about money?

   If someone makes me feel financially unsuccessful, I can get into fights about money.

33. Do you tend to get into arguments about religion?

   I try to stay away from that topic because it never goes well.

34. Do you tend to get into arguments about politics?

   Yes, I watch a lot of political television, and it gets me riled up. This topic has ruined many parties for me. It even causes fights between me and my girlfriend.

35. Do you tend to get into arguments about work?

   If I feel inadequate or criticized, yes, I get into arguments about work. When I think someone is insulting my work, I get furious.

36. Do you tend to get into arguments about family?

   Yes, I don't like it when people say bad things about anyone in my family, even though I have my own complaints about them. I'll fight anyone who criticizes my mom.

37. Do you tend to get into arguments about time?

   Oh yeah, this one is the WORST. My girlfriend is always on my case about being late. It's hard for me to finish what I'm doing so that we can leave the house on time. I don't know why she can't ever understand that.

PLACES

38. Are there certain places where you find yourself getting angry more often?

   For some reason, my girlfriend and I always fight when we're on a road trip in the car.

39. Where do you tend to have arguments? (Bedroom, living room, kitchen, yard, dining room, your in-law's house, etc.?)

We tend to fight in the kitchen. I guess if things are getting heated, we should get out of the kitchen fast.

40. Do you tend to get angry in your car?

I get mad if another driver cuts me off in traffic.

41. Do you tend to get angry at your place of employment?

I try to keep it to myself. Sometimes I feel mad at work, but I don't express it until I get home.

42. Do you tend to get angry while standing in queue?

Waiting in line pisses me off, but I can't do anything about it.

BODY SENSATIONS

43. What physical sensations do you tend to notice when you become angry?

My heart beats faster, my breathing is faster, my muscles clench.

44. Do you experience changes in body temperature, heart rate, muscle tension, digestion, respiration rate, salivation, perspiration, and/or diameter of the pupils?

I never thought about it before, but yes—I think sometimes my temperature changes, I lose my appetite, I sweat. . . .

45. Do you experience headaches, stomachaches, back or neck pain?

I get lots of headaches, lots of neck pain.

BEHAVIORS

46. What behaviors do you exhibit as you become angry?

At first I raise my voice, then I stomp around the house, sometimes I slam doors, and then at the end I usually leave the room—go off by myself to stew.

47. Do you "time travel"—meaning do you hold on to grudges, bring up the past, and/or review old offenses?

Yes—it's hard NOT to do that. Every time someone does something wrong, it makes me think of other times something like that happened. I get even angrier.

48. Do you slam doors, throw things, hit the wall, curse, scream, name-call, threaten, blame, sulk, or stew?

I slam doors, scream, threaten, blame, sulk, and stew. All of that.

49. Do you hit, grab, punch, shove, push, kick, spit, pinch, or bite?

No, but sometimes I want to.

50. Do you threaten others with weapons?

Never. But I think it's good that I don't own a gun. I'm afraid I would use a weapon if I had one in a moment of rage.

51. Do you threaten suicide or homicide?

No, I've never done that.

◆ TAMING YOUR TEMPER TIPS

Here are some simple tips for managing anger cycles and triggers when communicating with others. The list below contains the most common mistakes and their "fixes":

Stop saying, "Yeah, but..."

Saying things like, "yeah, but" can create polarization and put you at risk for engaging in a point-counterpoint argument. When you say "yeah, but," you are conveying defensiveness and justification. For instance, a husband might respond to his wife's complaint, "It feels like you're ignoring me," by saying, "Yeah, but I can't stand the way you nag me all the time."

- ✓ It's better to utilize a simple acknowledgment of the other person's side by saying, "Yes, and..."
- ✓ Express to the person, "I can see your perspective—it makes sense to me."
- ✓ Be willing to acknowledge your own defensiveness.
- ✓ Discover and acknowledge shared positions and viewpoints.
- ✓ Take time to listen so that you can consider different ideas.
- ✓ Respectfully disagree and be willing to give the other person time to consider your ideas.

Don't Over-Vent

Over-venting takes many forms such as nagging, yelling, tantrums, punching walls, or breaking things. It is important to express your feelings, but over-venting is counterproductive.

- ✓ Pay attention to your negative thoughts and to the feelings that arise from those thoughts. For example, when you think, "She's selfish" and "She doesn't care about my feelings," these types of thoughts can lead to over-venting.
- ✓ Utilize the "Time-Out" principles in order to prevent nagging, yelling, and tantrums.
- ✓ Stay away from unhealthy physical over-venting. Breaking dishes, punching walls, and violence are all physical expressions of over-venting.

Check Your Attitude

Sometimes people do not have a "communication problem"—they have an *attitude problem*. A common mistake people make is that they are communicating with crystal clarity, but their communication is bitter, rigid, disrespectful, and unloving in content or tone.

- ✓ Don't say something rude and offensive and then declare, "I'm just being honest!"
- ✓ Don't be so focused on getting your point across that you forget to be respectful.
- ✓ Approach the conversation with a collaborative mind-set, not a win-lose mentality.
- ✓ Remember not to let your tone overwhelm your content.
- ✓ Do not be punitive or judging.

Listen First, Solve Second

If you are trying to discuss a problem and the other person cuts you off by suggesting solutions, you often will not feel heard or understood. Situations such as these can lead to frustration and anger. When someone approaches you with a problem, hear them out first without leaping to offer solutions.

- ✓ Remember that when someone wants to talk about a problem, he or she usually just wants to be heard.
- ✓ Be a listener, not an idea-generator.
- ✓ Don't say, "Why don't you just (solution)?" People ask this question in order to cut the conversation short. Offering a "quick fix" generally makes the other person feel discounted or dismissed.
- ✓ Participate in the conversation by actively listening—by making eye contact, facing the person, reflecting what you hear, and asking questions.
- ✓ Provide solutions and options only when the other person is asking for them.

◈ HOW TO CONTROL YOUR ANGER CYCLES AND TRIGGERS

A toolkit of behavioral techniques will interrupt your anger cycle and anger triggers before they escalate into disaster. The strategies that follow will strengthen your ability to manage your anger constructively.

Time-Out and Self-Contract—Time-out helps you stop the Anger Cycle by creating a plan, paying attention to your anger signals, initiating a time-out, and using your time-out period productively. It also teaches you how to return to a discussion with a more open and productive approach.

How Your Body Responds to Anger—Anger triggers lead to physiological responses. The exercises show you how to use deep breathing, physical exercise, and visualization to help deal with your anger in healthier physical ways.

Successful Coping—Your first experiences of coping with stress and anger occurred when you were a child. To create a more successful coping style for the future, you start by remembering what worked well in the past. This exercise will explore past experiences in which you successfully managed conflict.

Request Forgiveness—Forgiveness is a critical component in short-circuiting the anger cycle. This exercise teaches you how to request forgiveness, deliver a proper apology, follow through on commitments made during the apology—and, just as important, forgive yourself.

FIVE STEPS TO AN EFFECTIVE TIME-OUT

When a situation gets heated, it is wise to take a break to give yourself time to cool off and evaluate it. You can create a time-out plan with a friend, family member, boyfriend, girlfriend, or spouse. Create this plan during a calm period time rather than in the heat of the moment. In order to have a successful time-out, follow these five steps:

STEP 1: CREATE A TIME-OUT PLAN TOGETHER.

- Come up with and agree on a "cue word" to signal the fact that you are reaching a level of anger that requires a time-out.

- Agree on the places you will go during your time-out.

- Decide how long you need for a full time-out and commit to return at an agreed-upon time.

- Commit to using your time apart to do some constructive analysis of the problem, to take responsibility for your own behavior, and to generate positive solutions.

- Agree to return at a specific time and a neutral place to discuss the problem calmly and constructively, without avoidance or further escalation.

STEP 2: NOTICE YOUR ANGER SIGNALS.

These signals may include:

- Yelling
- Glaring
- Interrupting
- Cursing
- Name-calling
- Threatening
- Pointing
- Slamming doors
- Sarcasm
- Criticizing
- Sighing
- Eye-rolling
- Lecturing

STEP 3: INITIATE A TIME-OUT.

A) First, use your "cue word" (It can be anything: "Poodle," "Uncle," even "Time-out".)

B) Follow up your cue word by saying something like, "I feel like I'm getting angry and I want to be fair to you, so please let me take a 35-minute break. I will meet back with you in the kitchen to resolve our argument." OR "I respect you, and I want to hear what you have to say. I think I can do that better if I take some time to calm down and then meet with you in your office."

STEP 4: USE YOUR TIME-OUT PERIOD PRODUCTIVELY.

A) Utilize empathy to better understand the other person's perspective about the issue or problem.

- Clarify your own position as well as the other person's position.
- Review your own coping strategies as well as the other person's coping strategies.
- Clarify your own needs and think about what the other person might need.
- Explore your own fears and try to imagine what the other person's fears might be.

B) Come up with an activity to help you calm down. Physical activity will help your body process the adrenaline in your system. Here are some ideas:

- Walking
- Biking
- Push-ups
- Weightlifting
- Aerobics
- Swimming

C) Generate some positive thoughts.

- Try to consider the whole story, not just your side.
- Remind yourself of what the other person has done right in regard to the problem.
- Focus on the good intentions on both sides.
- Remember that a person can love you without always agreeing with you.
- Remember that differences of opinion are not bad.
- Keep in mind that other variables could be influencing the discussion (past experiences, current mood, outside stressors, etc.).
- Realize the other person is not the enemy but, rather, is your teammate.
- Reaffirm your own desire to come to a mutually agreeable solution.

D) Stay away from these thoughts and behaviors:

- Stewing or ruminating
- Blaming
- Entitlement ("It should be my way. I should get what I want.")
- Rigid thinking and perfectionism
- Wanting to be right at all costs
- Reviewing a list of past grievances or offenses

- Drinking alcohol or doing drugs

STEP 5: AFTER THE TIME-OUT

- Honor your agreed-upon return time.
- Make sure that you choose a neutral environment for negotiation. For instance, if you tend to have more heated fights in the kitchen and more constructive conversations in the living room, remember to choose the living room as your safe zone where you will meet after your time-out.
- Listen without interrupting.
- Keep a normal tone of voice.
- Be prepared to compromise.
- Return to the conversation with some possible solutions.

DOES IT WORK?

Don't be surprised if time-out doesn't work for you right away. For many people, it takes a few tries because it's very hard to break habits. For example, when I explained time-out to one couple I worked with, they managed to continue bickering even about the time-out itself. Marge and Joe had been married for eight years and had a young child. Marge worked at a big discount store, and Joe was a plumber. The big fight they had almost daily was about how they spent their nonwork time. Joe always wanted to go fishing, and Marge wanted him to hang out with her and their son at her parents' house. Their fights were brutal. She would slam doors, and they'd go for days without speaking to each other. Their record was 14 days of cold, bitter silence. But one day when they started their usual fight, they agreed to a time-out that would not last more than one hour. Joe took a ride on his four-wheeler, and Marge exercised while he was out. Once he was out in the woods, Joe got his head straight enough to realize, oh, she's not really my enemy. She's not trying to keep me away from activities I love. They were able to come back and talk constructively. They came up with a great compromise: to start a little garden at Marge's mother's house. Joe loves the outdoors, Marge got to visit her mother, they spent time together gardening, and both of their needs were met.

TIME-OUT CONTRACT

The Time-Out Contract works in conjunction with Five Steps to an Effective Time-Out. It will help you commit to taking a break from angry situations so that you can cool off, think more clearly, and resolve problems more constructively.

A Time-Out Contract is a document you write describing how you will behave during a situation when anger begins to escalate. It does not require that another person commit to the same set of rules. You agree to follow the rules yourself as a way to manage your anger and do not spend time judging or critiquing the other party's method for managing anger. You simply adhere to your own contract.

EXERCISE 9: YOUR TIME-OUT CONTRACT

I agree to sit down with the person I have been struggling with and create the following Time-Out Plan:
See the *Jumpstart Exercise to help you complete this exercise.*

- **Time-Out Signal.** If I feel my anger rising to an unproductive level, I agree to use a Time-Out Signal. My Time-Out Signal will be: _____

- **Time-Out Duration.** My Time-Out will last for _____minutes. I commit to returning to the conversation immediately after this time period has passed.

- **Anger Escalation Identification.** I commit to noticing my own anger signals, such as the ones listed below:

- **Time-Out Productivity.** When I give my Time-Out Signal, here is what I commit to doing:

I COMMIT TO THESE RULES FOR WHAT I WILL DO DURING THE TIME-OUT:

- No driving
- No drinking alcohol or doing drugs
- No gossiping to other people about the dispute
- No stewing and/or working myself back up into an angrier state
- No focusing on resentments
- No hitting, no kicking, no door-slamming, no wall-punching, no physical violence
- Spending the time processing my own feelings and working through them

I COMMIT TO THESE RULES ONCE THE TIME-OUT IS OVER:

- Talk calmly about my own feelings and perceptions
- Own up to my own role in the conflict
- Avoid blaming, accusing, berating the other person
- Be willing to collaborate and come to a resolution

Signed :_____

Date :_____

Jumpstart the Exercise: Bob's Example

I agree to sit down with the person I have been struggling with and create the following Time-Out Plan:

- **Time-Out Signal.** If I feel my anger rising to an unproductive level, I agree to use a Time-Out Signal. My Time-Out Signal will be:
  Saying, "I think I need a break" along with the football hand symbol "T" for Time-Out

- **Time-Out Duration.** My time-out will last for *30* minutes. I commit to returning to the conversation immediately after this time period has passed.

- **Anger Escalation Identification.** I commit to noticing my own anger signals, such as the ones listed below:
  1. *I have angry, critical thoughts.*
  2. *I start to feel misunderstood, frustrated, and/or impatient.*
  3. *I raise my voice.*
  4. *My neck starts to hurt—I rub the back of my neck.*
  5. *I begin to feel hot—I might sweat.*
  6. *I feel my heart racing.*

- **Time-Out Productivity.** When I give my Time-Out Signal, here is what I commit to doing:
  I will go off into another room to spend some time thinking about how to do a better job of being accountable for my role in the problem, understanding other perspectives, and resolving the conflict.

I COMMIT TO THESE RULES FOR WHAT I WILL DO DURING THE TIME-OUT:

- No driving
- No drinking alcohol or doing drugs
- No gossiping to other people about the dispute
- No stewing and/or working myself back up into an angrier state
- No focusing on resentments
- No hitting, no kicking, no door-slamming, no wall-punching, no physical violence
- Spending the time processing my own feelings and working through them

I COMMIT TO THESE RULES ONCE THE TIME-OUT IS OVER:

- Talk calmly about my own feelings and perceptions
- Own up to my own role in the conflict
- Avoid blaming, accusing, berating the other person
- Be willing to collaborate and come to a resolution

Signed: *Robert William Everyman*   Date: *January 1, 2012*

HOW YOUR BODY RESPONDS TO ANGER

When you are angry your heart begins to beat faster, your need for oxygen increases, your adrenaline surges, your breathing becomes more rapid, your blood pressure increases, your muscles tense, and your body's energy activates. This activation causes you to search for a tension-release mechanism, such as slamming doors, punching walls, throwing objects, screaming, or physically assaulting someone.

I once had a client with life-threatening road rage. Max would blow his horn and give people the middle finger all the time. He followed a car into a parking lot to confront a person who was driving too slowly. When a driver moved into Max's lane without using a blinker, he got into a fistfight with the guy. I worked on helping him understand his biological response to anger and practice relaxation strategies to short-circuit that response.

Biologically, your "command and control center" is the autonomic nervous system. It regulates your involuntary physiological responses, such as heart rate, digestion, respiration, salivation, and pupil diameter.

The sympathetic nervous system activates the body's resources during times of fear, excitement, and anger, resulting in the "fight or flight" response. The "fight or flight" response is a direct result of an adrenaline rush produced by your body.

The sympathetic nervous system operates at all times to maintain physiological stability. It's your body's natural coping response for the normal stressors of daily activities as well as for the unexpected demands of urgent situations.

When you find yourself in the middle of a "fight or flight" response, it is important to process the adrenaline in your body. Below is a three-step process to metabolize adrenaline and deal with "fight or flight."

Step 1: Deep Breathing

When angry, most people tend to breathe from the chest rather than from the abdomen. Abdominal breathing allows more oxygen to come into the lungs and helps create a sense of calm. In order to manage your "fight or flight" response, slow down your respiration and breathe more deeply. Start by finding a comfortable place that is quiet and calm.

Lie on your back or stand up straight. Place one hand on your abdominal area and one hand on your chest. Now breathe. Determine what area rises and falls more noticeably. If your chest rises more than your belly, then you will need to spend some time teaching yourself how to breathe from your abdomen.

Inhale slowly through your nose and focus on allowing your belly to expand. Your chest should only move slightly. Exhale through your mouth. This step helps maximize the amount of oxygen in your body.

Focus on slowing down the pace of your breathing. Inhale through your nose for 3 seconds. Hold your breath for 2 seconds, and then exhale through your mouth for 5 seconds. Think of this as the 3-2-5 Rule.

Now practice your abdominal breathing for 10 minutes.

The next time you are angry, pay attention to your breathing. The depth and rhythm of your breath can serve to override the "fight or flight" response. Implement abdominal breathing and the 3-2-5 rule the next time you feel your anger escalating. If you find that your anger levels remain high after this deep breathing exercise, move on to Step 2.

Step 2: Releasing Muscle Tension

When you become angry, you experience muscle tension as part of the "fight or flight" response. If you can become more aware of the areas where you hold chronic muscle tension and learn to release it, you will feel more in charge of your anger. While you are focusing on relaxing your muscle groups, you are not likely to simultaneously ruminate and escalate in anger.

When you find your levels of anger rising, focus on where in your body you feel muscle tension accumulating. For example, you might feel tension in your neck, back, or shoulders.

As you begin to focus on those areas of tension, implement your deep breathing skills.

Next, drop your head forward and roll it gently clockwise and then again, slowly, counterclockwise.

Now lift your shoulders up, as if you are trying to touch your ears. Hold your shoulders in place for 3 seconds.

Then release, dropping your shoulders back down again. Repeat 2–3 times.

As you take a deep breath, gently arch your back, while pushing your abdomen out. Hold this position and then release. Lean forward and try to touch your toes. Repeat back-arch exercise.

Lie flat on your back with your knees bent; lift your buttocks off the floor, squeeze and hold. Next, release and lower your buttocks back down to the floor. Repeat 3 times.

Now extend your legs out horizontally. Flex your toes toward your calves. Contract your thigh and calf muscles, and hold for 5 seconds. Then release.

Find a comfortable place to sit or lie down. Close your eyes. Imagine that you feel calm and that your anger has melted away. Imagine your favorite place to be—somewhere quiet, beautiful, and peaceful. Allow yourself to see the beauty of this imagined environment, and to smell, hear, touch, and taste all of the sensations that accompany your favorite place. Remember what it feels like to be there and to be relaxed.

AFFIRMATIONS

You can decrease your muscle tension through positive affirmation self-talk.

Remind yourself, "I can handle anger effectively and calmly," "I have the ability to cope with stress and anger," and "I feel competent to manage my anger."

Tell yourself, "Anger is normal when handled in healthy ways," "I cannot control other people—I can only control myself," "It is healthy to apologize when I'm wrong," and "It is okay for me to be accountable for my own behavior."

The next time you're angry, pay attention to your muscle tension. Try tense-and-release exercises anytime you find yourself becoming angry. These exercises will help discharge accumulated muscle tension. If you find that your anger levels remain high after this releasing muscle tension exercise, move on to Step 3.

Step 3: Physical Exercise

Exercise can help you process the adrenaline response that occurs when you are angry. Exercise also gives you a break from the event, gives you time to think more clearly, and helps you feel better in general. Here are some healthy options:

- Take a 30-minute walk
- Do 20 push-ups
- Do 20 sit-ups
- Go for a 1-mile run
- Lift weights
- Go to an aerobics or martial arts class
- Do swim laps
- Use a treadmill or stationary bike
- Ride your bike
- Jump rope
- Do yoga
- Do yard work or gardening
- Do active household chores (vacuum, wash windows, do dishes, etc.)
- Put on some music and dance

- Walk your dog
- Play basketball
- Go to the batting cages and practice
- Play golf
- Go rollerblading
- Wash the car

You've learned three ways to manage anger physically: Deep breathing, releasing muscle tension, and physical exercise. Now you can begin to practice what you have discovered about how the body processes anger. See the ***Jumpstart Exercise to help you complete this exercise.***

EXERCISE 10: PHYSICAL MANAGEMENT OF ANGER

Deep Breathing Results

The next time you feel yourself getting angry, try using the deep breathing technique. After you experiment with deep breathing, check your results by answering the questions below:

1. What did you notice about your breathing that made you know you were getting angry?

2. At what point did you decide to implement the deep breathing technique?

3. Was the exercise helpful to you?

4. What happened after you finished the exercise?

5. Could you feel a difference in your levels of anger?

Releasing Muscle Tension

Once you have finished the deep breathing exercise, you can try releasing muscle tension if you still feel that your anger levels are too high. Check your results by answering the following questions:

1. How did you notice within your muscles that you were becoming angry?

2. At what point did you decide to implement releasing muscle tension?

3. Was the exercise helpful to you?

4. What happened after you finished the exercise?

5.   Could you feel a difference in your levels of anger?

Physical Exercise

After you experiment with physical exercise, check your results by answering these questions:

1.   How did you notice within your body that you were becoming angry?

2.   At what point did you decide to implement physical exercise?

3.   Was the physical exercise helpful to you?

4.   What happened after you finished the physical exercise?

5.   Could you feel a difference in your levels of anger?

Jumpstart the Exercise: Bob's Example

Deep Breathing

1. What did you notice about your breathing that made you know you were getting angry?

   I could feel my breathing getting shallower and faster, and it was coming from up higher in my body.

2. At what point did you decide to implement the deep breathing technique?

   As I noticed myself becoming angry, I remembered what I had learned about breathing and how it affects the nervous system. Before I let my anger go any further, I decided to try deep breathing.

3. Was the exercise helpful to you?

   Yes, it was. At first I felt a little silly, but then I decided I liked the idea of being able to gain control of my body in a somewhat short period of time. It was simple, so it didn't feel like a big deal to try doing it.

4. What happened after you finished the exercise?

   I was still angry, of course, but I could feel my anger drain away to a more manageable level. I felt like I could handle it—like I could face it without losing control.

5. Could you feel a difference in your levels of anger?

   Yes, I was noticeably less angry after doing the deep breathing. It didn't erase my anger, but it helped me manage it.

Releasing Muscle Tension

1. How did you notice within your muscles that you were becoming angry?

   I could feel my neck becoming tense, my fists were clenching, and I was gritting my teeth.

2. At what point did you decide to implement releasing muscle tension?

   I tried it after the deep breathing exercise. After the deep breathing, my muscles were not as tense, but they still felt somewhat tight. I thought I would just test out the exercise to see if it helped.

3. Was the exercise helpful to you?

   Yes, it gave me something to think about besides the thing that was making me mad, it helped me not to stew about it, and it gave me time to calm down.

4. What happened after you finished the exercise?

   Afterward, I felt a bit calmer than before, my muscles were less tense, and I felt a little more able to think clearly. At that point, I tried some of the visualization and affirmations. I thought about what it feels like when I'm on the beach. I said to myself, "I cannot control other people—I can only control myself." I also told myself, "It is healthy to apologize when I'm wrong."

5. Could you feel a difference in your levels of anger?

   Yes, I still felt angry but not furious like before. I also felt more open to the idea that I might have some responsibility for my part of the argument. I was more willing to consider looking at my own behavior.

Physical Exercise

1. How did you notice within your body that you were becoming angry?

   I noticed it earlier when my breathing changed and my muscles clenched up. Even after doing the other experiments, I could still feel that there was some negative energy stored in my body.

2. At what point did you decide to implement physical exercise?

   I decided to try exercise after doing the deep breathing and releasing muscle tension—just to see how much better I could feel if I went ahead and did the physical exercise too.

3. Was the physical exercise helpful to you?

   Yes, I did 20 push-ups and then I took the dog for a brisk walk. I think it helped me. I could feel my body respond to the physical activity.

4. What happened after you finished the physical exercise?

   I felt much calmer than before. My anger was much, much lower, I had better perspective on the problem, and I began to realize that I was blowing things out of proportion at the beginning of the conflict. I felt like I could talk things out more rationally after my walk.

5. Could you feel a difference in your levels of anger?

   Yes, my anger was drastically reduced. I'm going to try to do this when I start to feel my anger escalating from now on.

EXERCISE 11: SUCCESSFUL COPING IN YOUR PAST

I'm sure you have not failed miserably at coping with anger every single time you have ever experienced it. Think back: Have you logged some moments when you got mad, coped successfully, and felt reasonably good about it? If you can remember what has worked in the past, odds are that it might work again. At the least, you will have a good starting point from which to launch your new efforts at improved coping. See the **Jumpstart Exercise to help you complete this exercise.**

1. As a child, can you remember a time when you got mad and resolved it peacefully? Describe that time.

2. As a teenager, can you recall a situation where you were able to reduce your anger without yelling, making a scene, stomping off in a huff, or resorting to a physical display? What did you do?

3. As a young adult, can you recall an angry exchange that you handled with diplomacy? What did you say? How did you say it?

4. As a mature adult, can you remember resolving a disagreement with wisdom and patience? How did that happen? What did you do to maintain your composure?

5. In your work environment, have you ever handled a dispute professionally and courteously? How did you cope with your angry feelings? What did you do to stay calm?

Jumpstart the Exercise: Ted's Example

1. As a child, can you remember a time when you got mad and resolved it peacefully? Describe that time.

   I can remember being very angry with a boy in our neighborhood who had stolen my football. I confronted him in the yard and asked him to give it back. I didn't yell or beat him up—I just waited for him to give me the football, and he did. I remember being surprised. I usually had to fight for anything I wanted when I was a kid.

2. As a teenager, can you recall a situation where you were able to reduce your anger without yelling, making a scene, stomping off in a huff, or resorting to a physical display? What did you do?

   When I was 14, my English teacher gave me an unfair grade on an essay. I was very angry and wanted to yell at her, but instead I wrote a note letting her know five reasons why I disagreed with the grade on the essay. She didn't change my grade, but later she explained to me how her grading system worked. It helped me to be less mad when I understood why my grade looked so low. It also helped me explain the grade to my parents so that I wouldn't get into so much trouble.

3. As a young adult, can you recall an angry exchange that you handled with diplomacy? What did you say? How did you say it?

   I remember being in my 20s and having to deal with creditors who were bothering me about my student loans. I did get curt and unfriendly with them, but I also got motivated to consolidate my debt. Now I'm in a much better position financially.

4. As a mature adult, can you remember resolving a disagreement with wisdom and patience? How did that happen? What did you do to maintain your composure?

   When I turned 30, I had an argument with the contractor who was working on my house. I wanted to hit him—I was so furious about all of the shoddy workmanship and all the time delays. Instead of punching him, I let him know that I would not pay him for work that wasn't completed. I stopped giving him checks, and he got back to work.

5. In your work environment, have you ever handled a dispute professionally and courteously? How did you cope with your angry feelings? What did you do to stay calm?

   I do have a temper, but I've held my temper at work pretty well. Last year, I was given a work schedule that I didn't want. I was informed I would be working on the night shift for a full two years. I was enraged—especially since I had so much seniority. It didn't seem right to me. Before I blew up at my boss, I told him my concerns. He explained that they needed one experienced trainer on the night shift and that they trusted me. I told him I appreciated it, but that I preferred to work the day shift. He reconsidered and changed my schedule back to the old one. I was very grateful and told him so. After the fact, I was so glad that I hadn't charged into his office and made a scene.

REQUESTING FORGIVENESS

Why is it important to apologize? Anger often results in hard feelings and, when left unresolved, makes people become bitter and resentful, and hold grudges. Requesting forgiveness shows accountability, empathy, and respect, bringing relief, self-respect, and resolution.

DELIVER A PROPER APOLOGY

- Remember to say the actual words, "I'm sorry" or "I apologize," but don't leave it at that. Give examples: Not just "Sorry." Say something like, "I'm sorry I broke your favorite crystal bowl. I know it has special meaning to you, because your brother gave it to you just before he passed away."

- Be kind.

- Avoid defensiveness. Never say, "I'm sorry, but . . ."—It nullifies the apology.

- Be accountable for the things you did wrong.

- Be open to listening to feedback, in case you missed something or left something out.

- Leave your ego at the door.

- Be willing to endeavor not to repeat the mistake. Commit to making changes.

- Don't "Apologize to Appease." Empty, repeated apologies can come across as dismissive and unsympathetic.

FOLLOWING THROUGH ON PROMISES

- Once you have explained that you will try not to repeat the mistake, the focus must now turn to how you will follow through on those commitments.

- Do not promise more than you can deliver.

- After apologizing—commit to one small step, rather than overreaching and feeling like a failure

- Hold yourself accountable for following through

- Do not procrastinate or avoid making changes

FORGIVE YOURSELF

If your conscience is bothering you and you cannot seem to forgive yourself, then you might have to go a step further:

- Work off your guilt. You can convey your regret by doing nice things for the person you hurt, being more available, offering to help, and so on.

- If you have already been forgiven and there is nothing left to repair, then you can transfer your "working it off" plan to someone on the sidelines or even a total stranger. A few hours in a soup kitchen might give you a new outlook.

- Take an inventory of what you have learned—welcome the lessons and apply them in your life.

- Value yourself and the progress you have made up to this point.
- Offer empathy to yourself—appreciate both your strengths and your limitations.
- Accept your own humanness—make room for imperfection and growth.

EXERCISE 12: YOUR APOLOGY

See the *Jumpstart Exercise to help you complete this exercise.*

1. Think about a recent argument. Now compose your own proper apology:

2. In the argument you referenced above, what commitments do you need to make in order not to repeat the mistake?

3. How will you hold yourself accountable to following through on these commitments?

4. Have you forgiven yourself for the argument you described above?

5. If you haven't forgiven yourself completely, what do you need to do in order to feel satisfied that you have done everything you need to do to demonstrate your regret?

6. What actions do you need to take in order to complete the apology?

7. Take an inventory—what have you learned?

8. What do you see in yourself that shows you have made progress? How can you show yourself empathy?

Jumpstart the Exercise: John's Example

1. Think about a recent argument. Now compose your own proper apology:

   My girlfriend was upset because I forgot to call her one night when I stayed late at an office party. I said, "You have to get over your jealousy, I just got distracted." I could have apologized to her by saying, "I apologize for forgetting to call. I imagine it made you worry about me. It was thoughtless and I don't intend to let it happen again. From now on, I'll stop leaving my cell phone in the car. I'll have it with me so that I can text you to let you know I'll be late."

2. In the argument you referenced above, what commitments do you need to make in order not to repeat the mistake?

   I am committing not to leave my phone in the car. I am promising to text my girlfriend when I'm running late.

3. How will you hold yourself accountable to following through on these commitments?

   I'm going to install a "reminder function" on my phone for times when I'm going to be out at functions without my girlfriend. I'll hear a "ping" to remind me to text her if it gets past 10 P.M. I don't want her to worry.

4. Have you forgiven yourself for the argument you described above?

   Only partly.

5. If you haven't forgiven yourself completely, what do you need to do in order to feel satisfied that you have done everything you need to do to demonstrate your regret?

   I need to make sure that I tell my girlfriend that I remember our plan for how to avoid this problem in the future—I don't want her to think I forgot that we came up with a solution.

6. What actions do you need to take in order to complete the apology?

   If I continue to feel guilty, I'll talk more with my girlfriend about it. Also, if I do something nice for my girlfriend or even for a stranger, I might feel better about myself.

7. Take an inventory—what have you learned?

   I've learned that sometimes I get caught up in the moment and that I temporarily forget about common courtesies. If I make a plan ahead of time, I can avoid creating problems in my relationship. I've also learned that my girlfriend worries about me when I don't show up—she notices when I'm not there.

8. What do you see in yourself that shows you have made progress? How can you show yourself empathy?

   I'm not perfect, but I have made a genuine effort to repair the problem and to prevent it from happening in the future. I think that says a lot.

CHAPTER THREE

Family History And Relationships

Have you ever stopped to wonder where your anger comes from and how it affects the way you manage it? My client Julie is a 30-year-old woman who came to me because she was treating her husband so badly and didn't have a clue about why. She talks down to him, tells him he's stupid, and he can't seem to do anything right. Recently they had a new baby girl, and she sent him out to buy diapers. When he came back with the toddler size, Julie lit into him, berating him for not knowing a newborn couldn't possibly fit into a toddler size. After talking with her for a while, I discovered Julie had grown up with a verbally abusive mother. No matter how hard Julie tried, nothing she did was ever good enough for her perfectionist parent. As she told me she still works with her mother in the family's diner, a light bulb went off in Julie's mind. "Oh my god," Julie said, "I see—I'm becoming my mom!"

If parents, or others who influence us as children, model poor anger management skills, then we copy them. We do what we have seen others do or what we have been taught to do until we learn something new. By examining your history and influences, you will improve your anger management skills. Insight creates awareness and builds better relationships. You can also learn new strategies to change your approach in current relationships. Keep in mind that it may be painful to relive your childhood. There's usually a good reason you haven't wanted to look too closely. But if you hold out the carrot of taming your temper, you will be motivated to keep chipping away. You will be surprised to find how much you can learn by thinking carefully about your family history.

EXERCISE 13: YOUR FAMILY HISTORY

See the ***Jumpstart Exercise to help you complete this exercise.*** Explore your family history of managing anger by answering these questions:

PARENT/GUARDIAN ONE

1. How did parent one express anger? (e.g., did he/she throw objects, scream, name-call, and slam doors)

2. What was this parent's coping strategy after a conflict? (e.g., did he/she shut down, isolate, fight back, or consume alcohol or food)

3. Was your parent able to resolve conflict successfully? How or how not?

PARENT/GUARDIAN TWO

4. How did parent two express anger? (e.g., did he/she throw objects, scream, name-call, and slam doors)

5. What was this parent's coping strategy after a conflict? (e.g., did he/she shut down, isolate, fight back, or consume alcohol or food)

6. Was your parent able to resolve conflict successfully? How or how not?

PARENTS, STEPPARENTS, GUARDIANS

7. When your parents were mad at each other, what happened?

8. How did your parents resolve conflict?

9. What is the angriest episode you have ever witnessed in your family?

SIBLINGS

10. How did your siblings express anger? (e.g., did they throw objects, scream, name-call, and slam doors)

11. What were their coping strategies after a conflict? (e.g., did they shut down, isolate, fight back, or consume alcohol or food)

12. Were your siblings able to resolve conflict successfully? How or how not?

YOUR ANGER

13. What is your first memory of anger as a child?

14. What were you thinking in the moment?

15. What were you feeling in the moment?

16. How did you behave in the moment?

17. Are there similarities between how you were treated as a child and how you treat others presently?

18. Have you incorporated your family's anger styles into your own style? (e.g., did they throw objects, scream, name-call, and slam doors and now do you do the same?)

19. How has your family's anger style affected your own adult beliefs about anger? (e.g., "Anger is bad," "Anger is unhealthy," and "Anger is destructive.")

Jumpstart the Exercise: Carlos's Example

PARENT/GUARDIAN ONE

1. How did parent one express anger? (e.g., did he/she throw objects, scream, name-call, and slam doors)

   My mom expressed anger by yelling and slamming doors. Once I saw her throw a plate.

2. What was this parent's coping strategy after a conflict? (e.g., did he/she shut down, isolate, fight back, or consume alcohol or food?)

   After a conflict, my mom always went shopping to "treat herself."

3. Was your parent able to resolve conflict successfully? How or how not?

    My mom's conflicts usually bubbled back up to the surface a day or two later. She would explode, shop, and then explode again—she would do this when she was mad at us, at someone else, or at my stepdad.

PARENT/GUARDIAN TWO

4. How did parent two express anger? (e.g., did he/she throw objects, scream, name-call, and slam doors?)

    My dad is deceased, but my stepdad is still living. My stepdad expressed anger by giving my mom the silent treatment.

5. What was this parent's coping strategy after a conflict? (e.g., did he/she shut down, isolate, fight back, or consume alcohol or food)

    My stepdad coped by spending a lot of time alone. After a fight, he would retreat to the garage and sit out there smoking and drinking beer.

6. Was your parent able to resolve conflict successfully? How or how not?

    He never really did. When my mom would tell him how she felt, my stepdad would shut down. Then my mom would go to the mall, and the cycle would start all over again.

PARENTS, STEPPARENTS, GUARDIANS

7. When your parents were mad at each other, what happened?

    My mom would yell, and my stepdad would give her the silent treatment. My mom retaliated by using her credit card.

8. How did your parents resolve conflict?

    They didn't. Not in a healthy way.

9. What is the angriest episode you have ever witnessed in your family?

    One time, my stepdad found a new, expensive dress in the back of my mom's closet with the price tag still attached. He hit the roof. This argument took on epic proportions, probably because they had never really resolved the earlier fight, which had led to my mom buying the designer dress in the first place. The fight escalated. My stepdad was cold. He accused my mom of buying the dress so that she could look pretty for our next-door neighbor, who was a bachelor.

    My mom was shocked at the accusation. My stepdad stomped out of the room and into the garage. As the doorway from the kitchen to the garage closed; my mom threw a plate at his head. It missed. There's still a dent in the paint on that door to this day. My mom never wore that fancy dress.

SIBLINGS

10. How did your siblings express anger? (e.g., did they throw objects, scream, name-call, and slam doors?)

    My sister screamed and stomped her feet. She huffed around the house.

11. What were their coping strategies after a conflict? (e.g., did they shut down, isolate, fight back, or consume alcohol or food?)

I only have one sister—and she copes after a fight by telling and retelling her side of the story to as many people as she can. She holds grudges.

12. Were your siblings able to resolve conflict successfully? How or how not?

Sometimes I admired the fact that my sister was able to express her feelings so well after a fight when she was talking to her friends. However, I don't think she was very good at resolving conflict.

YOUR ANGER

13. What is your first memory of anger as a child?

I remember that my mom and my sister wanted to go shopping and I was forced to go with them. I wanted to go to the park, but no one would listen to me, so I pitched a tantrum in the middle of the mall.

14. What were you thinking in the moment?

I remember thinking, "No one cares about what <u>I want! No one listens to me!</u>"

15. What were you feeling in the moment?

I felt angry and frustrated because they were controlling me.

16. How did you behave in the moment?

I flipped out—I screamed, stomped, threw myself onto the floor of the mall and made sure that everyone could hear me.

17. Are there similarities between how you were treated as a child and how you treat others presently?

Maybe . . . I was treated okay sometimes, and other times it seems like I was expected to be okay with being ignored and yet also to tolerate a giant amount of high emotion in my family. People always seemed to be upset about something.—And now, I probably expect my girlfriend to tolerate being neglected while also putting up with monumental amounts of negative emotion from me.

18. Have you incorporated your family's anger styles into your own style? (e.g., did they throw objects, scream, name-call, and slam doors and now do you do the same?)

Yes, I do think I can be impulsive and loud like my mom, defensive like my sister, and from time to time I go silent like my stepdad.

19. How has your family's anger style affected your own adult beliefs about anger? (e.g., "Anger is bad," "Anger is unhealthy," and "Anger is destructive.")

Sometimes I think, "Anger is Power—it makes me a tough guy," but other times I think, "Anger is bad, and it doesn't get you anywhere"—so I don't really know what I think.

HISTORY OF ABUSE

Those of you who have suffered abuse probably know how dramatically it's shaped the way you handle your relationships. Abuse has an impact on your self-concept, thoughts, feelings, and behaviors. It can make you passive or very aggressive. As you answer these questions, think about how past abuse affects your current anger.

If you have a history of physical, emotional, or sexual abuse, then it is important for you to seek help from a qualified professional counselor. This workbook is not a substitute for therapy. Find a therapist who specializes in issues of trauma and abuse and make an appointment as soon as possible.

EXERCISE 14: YOUR HISTORY OF ABUSE

See the *Jumpstart Exercise to help you complete this exercise.*
Answer the questions below about your own possible abuse history:

1. Were you physically abused?

2. Were you emotionally abused?

3. Were you sexually abused?

4. Was there any substance abuse in your family?

5. How has past abuse affected your anger?

6. How has past abuse affected your thoughts about yourself?

1. Were you physically abused?

   I was spanked as a child, and once my stepdad hit me hard with a belt.

2. Were you emotionally abused?

   I'm not sure. . . .I think it would have helped if my parents had cared more about my feelings, but they just didn't do that.

3. Were you sexually abused?

   No, I wasn't, but my girlfriend was, and I know it must have been hard for her growing up. Even now, it has an effect on her.

4. Was there any substance abuse in your family?

   No drugs, but I do think my stepdad drank beer to escape his feelings. He also smoked a lot.

5. How has past abuse affected your anger?

   It's possible that I am an angrier person now than I would have been if I had felt more cared for as a child. I will never spank or hit my children because I don't think that physical punishment helped me at all when I was a kid.

6. How has past abuse affected your thoughts about yourself?

   I often feel ignored, unworthy of attention, and like I have to "look out for Number One."

RELATIONSHIP TECHNIQUES

Looking at your family history will help you gain insight into some of the most important relationships in your life. Just as past anger affected your relationships as a child, anger now has a significant impact on both your romantic and platonic relationships.

When you achieve mastery over your ability to handle your emotions, you are better equipped to be a loving, fair, and loyal partner and friend. In this section, you will acquire new skills to bring into partnerships.

ACCOUNTABILITY IN RELATIONSHIPS

Accountability means taking responsibility for one's own actions. Learning to be accountable by "owning up to" and "answering for" your actions is a major part of managing and resolving conflict. When two people argue, fights often escalate when one or both people refuse to be accountable. This creates a "Me versus You" mentality, and positions become entrenched. Common tactics that individuals utilize to avoid accountability are minimization, denial, and blame.

Taking responsibility for even a small part in a conflict can help you reach resolution. Even if you do not feel as if you are entirely at fault, it is highly likely that there is at least some portion of the argument where you have not behaved perfectly.

EXERCISE 15: YOUR ACCOUNTABILITY IN RELATIONSHIPS

This exercise will help you work toward healthier collaboration. It will assist you in learning how to improve your willingness to accept responsibility for your own role in creating, maintaining, and perpetuating conflict. In the end, accepting accountability can start the process of moving you away from conflict and toward resolution. See the *Jumpstart Exercise to help you complete the exercise.*

1. Think about the last major conflict you had in your relationship where you were NOT willing to be accountable for your side of the argument. Describe the conflict in the space below:

2. Both individuals should now admit to some points within the argument where they were not willing to accept reasonable accountability.

    a) How did you minimize your role in the conflict?

b) How did you deny responsibility?

c) How did you blame the other person?

3. Both individuals acknowledge their own roles in the conflict.

Person 1	Person 2
Thoughts about the conflict that kept you from being accountable?	Thoughts about the conflict that kept you from being accountable?
Feelings about the conflict that kept you from being accountable?	Feelings about the conflict that kept you from being accountable?
Behaviors within the conflict that kept you from being accountable?	Behaviors within the conflict that kept you from being accountable?

4. Both individuals take time to apologize for their offenses and for their earlier refusal to take responsibility.

PERSON 1:

- "I know my thoughts about _____ held me back from being responsible for my own role in the conflict."

- "I am aware that my feelings in regard to _____ made it hard for me to see your perspective."

- "The things I did in anger, such as _____, were not helpful in resolving the argument."

PERSON 2:

- "I know my thoughts about_____heldmebackfrombeingresponsible for my own role in the conflict."

- "I am aware that my feelings in regard to _____made it hard for me to see your perspective."

- "The things I did in anger, such as _____ were not helpful in resolving the argument."

Jumpstart the Exercise: Deb's Example

1. Think about the last major conflict you had in your relationship where you were NOT willing to be accountable for your side of the argument. Describe the conflict in the space below:

   DEB: I was very angry when I discovered that my mom planned a family vacation and did not include my live-in boyfriend.

   DEB's MOM: I planned a nice family vacation and suddenly Deb blew up at me, accusing me of hating her boyfriend. I didn't know where it came from or why she felt that way.

2. Both individuals should now admit to some points within the argument where they were not willing to accept reasonable accountability.

   a) How did you minimize your role in the conflict?

   DEB: I minimized my role in the conflict by blaming it all on my mother because she never communicated her plan to me ahead of time. I didn't ask questions or try to understand.

   DEB's MOM: I minimized my role in the conflict by refusing to acknowledge that I had done anything that might even SEEM disrespectful. I wasn't willing to see her point of view.

   b) How did you deny responsibility?

   DEB: I denied responsibility by shifting the focus to my mom's behavior. I focused on my resentment rather than thinking before I speak.

   DEB's MOM: I denied responsibility by being defensive and by not being willing to look at my own behavior from Deb's perspective.

   c) How did you blame the other person?

   DEB: I blamed my mom by accusing her of always wanting to exclude my boyfriend from family events. I blamed her for "making me angry."

   DEB's MOM: I blamed my Deb by accusing her of being crazy, explosive, and overreactive. In the end, I still believe Deb's behavior was wrong . . . but I also think I could have handled it better.

3. Both individuals acknowledge their own roles in the conflict.

Person 1: *Deb*	Person 2: *Deb's Mom*
Thoughts about the conflict that kept you from being accountable? *"She has never really accepted him"* *"My mom is inconsiderate"* *"She always pushes my buttons!"*	Thoughts about the conflict that kept you from being accountable? *"Deb is acting crazy"* *"What's her problem??"* *"She always explodes"*
Feelings about the conflict that kept you from being accountable? *Resentment* *Hurt* *Rage*	Feelings about the conflict that kept you from being accountable? *Confusion* *Fear* *Defensiveness*
Behaviors within the conflict that kept you from being accountable? *Refusing to calm down* *Behaving in an emotional manner—screaming, hanging up the phone, etc.* *Wanting to win the argument and not being willing to apologize, even when my mom was trying to talk calmly to me.*	Behaviors within the conflict that kept you from being accountable? *Not being willing to admit that I could have talked to Deb <u>before</u> I made the vacation reservation. Assuming that Deb would read my mind and know that I love her and don't want to hurt her*

4. Both individuals take time to apologize for their offenses and for their earlier refusal to take responsibility.

PERSON 1:
- "I know my thoughts about *you wanting to exclude my boyfriend, my inability to understand your motivations, and my assumption that you were trying to hurt me* held me back from being responsible for my own role in the conflict."
- "I am aware that my feelings in regard to *hurt, rage, and resentment* made it hard for me to see your perspective."
- "The things I did in anger, such as *behaving impulsively, shouting at you (not okay) and being too proud to apologize,* were not helpful in resolving the argument."

PERSON 2:
- "I know my thoughts about *Deb being crazy, Deb being over-reactive, and so on,* held me back from being responsible for my own role in the conflict."
- "I am aware that my feelings in regard to *confusion, fear, and defensiveness* made it hard for me to see your perspective."

- "The things I did in anger, such as *not admitting how I could have prevented the fight by verifying the travel plans in advance, refusing to see Deb's perspective, and assuming that Deb should "just know" that I love her and wouldn't want to hurt her* were not helpful in resolving the argument."

COMMUNICATION 101

Communication is about sending and receiving messages in our relationships. We learn about communication first in our families. Later we learn more about communication in school, with friends, at the workplace, and in our romantic partnerships. This exercise checks your current communication ability, reviews the fundamental components of communication, and helps you improve your basic communication skills.

Parents teach us how to tie our shoes, say please and thank you, button our shirts, do our chores, and brush our teeth. But few of us receive formal training on how to communicate our anger effectively. Parents might teach healthy communication in bits and pieces, but rarely in a thorough, comprehensive way.

Regardless of the topic, almost all problems can be traced back to communication. When we're angry, it is crucial to have healthy communication.

EXERCISE 16: COMMUNICATION CHECK

Check "Yes" or "No":

1. Are you unable to maintain a conversational tone during conflicts?

    ☐ Yes   ☐ No

2. Are you unable to show empathy or sensitivity during an argument?

    ☐ Yes   ☐ No

3. Do you tend to interrupt during discussions or conflicts?

    ☐ Yes   ☐ No

4. Do you struggle with compromising during an argument?

    ☐ Yes   ☐ No

5. Is it difficult for you to generate options and solutions when resolving a dispute?

    ☐ Yes   ☐ No

6. Are you unwilling to see other points of view?

    ☐ Yes   ☐ No

7. Do you threaten others to get your way?

    ☐ Yes   ☐ No

8. Do you apply *shoulds*, *oughts*, and *musts* to other people and their behavior?

    ☐ Yes   ☐ No

9. Do you teach, advise, lecture, or relentlessly use logic in order to influence or persuade?

    ☐ Yes   ☐ No

10. Do you yell and name-call?

    ☐ Yes   ☐ No

11. Do you withdraw from conflict?

    ☐ Yes   ☐ No

12. Do you grill the other person with questions like "when, where, how, who, and what?"

    ☐ Yes   ☐ No

13. Do you judge and criticize?

    ☐ Yes   ☐ No

14. Do you blame and accuse?

    ☐ Yes   ☐ No

15. Are you unable to admit your mistakes?

    ☐ Yes   ☐ No

Add up your total number of "Yes" answers. Look at the Scoring Key to get a general idea of your ability to communicate.

Test Scoring

THREAT LEVELS:

LEVEL YELLOW = 1–5— ELEVATED RISK FOR COMMUNICATION ERRORS

LEVEL ORANGE = 6–10— HIGH RISK FOR COMMUNICATION ERRORS

LEVEL RED = 11–15— SEVERE RISK FOR COMMUNICATION ERRORS

We all could stand to update or improve our communication skills from time to time. Regardless of which category you fall into, you could benefit from improving yours.

TWO BASIC COMMUNICATION SKILLS

We all have barriers that keep us from receiving the full content of the messages others are trying to send us. Some of these barriers include:

- Indulging in excessive internal chatter

- Coming up with counterarguments

- Ignoring parts of the message

- Being exhausted

- Being distracted by externals (television, radio, computer, video games)

- Experiencing fear (of criticism, of being rejected, of not being heard)

Excellent listeners know how to give their full attention to the message-sender by taking in all aspects of the message.

Excellent senders know how to communicate a message at all levels and are mindful of the impact the message has on the listener.

EXERCISE 17: TWO BASIC COMMUNICATION SKILLS

This exercise will teach you how to both listen and send messages well.

SKILL 1: LISTENING

Capturing What You Hear—Paying attention to the information being conveyed.

- Quiet the internal chatter by making yourself meet the other person's gaze, shifting your body to face the other person, and reminding yourself to slow down and listen to the actual words and verbal content of the message.

- When you catch yourself generating counterarguments while the other person is talking, remind yourself that the other person is not the enemy—that you share common goals, that the other person has a right to his or her own feelings. Let go of defensiveness by setting aside your own agenda—discipline yourself to become curious and take an interest in learning about the message being sent.

- Listen to the full content of the message without interrupting. Let the other person finish his or her complete thought and *then* give appropriate weight to all parts of the message.

- Assess your energy level and ask yourself, "Is now a good time for a difficult conversation?" Focus on self-care and on your own mental health. Know when to delay a conversation.

- Be mindful of regulating external distraction—eliminate television, radio, computer, and video games when you are entering into an important conversation.

- Courageously open yourself to hearing things you might not want to hear—the message being sent has the power to educate you, even if you feel uncomfortable with it. Learn to tolerate discomfort.

Capturing Nonverbal Messages—Noticing tone of voice, body posture, facial expressions, and gestures.

- Pay attention to volume.

- Notice the style and tone of communication. Is it conversational, inflated, flat, heated, anxious, or apathetic?

- Watch for body posture. Sometimes someone might lean closer to you when feeling interested in what you have to say, someone might recoil from you when feeling fearful or disgusted, or someone might slump in a chair when feeling defeated. Ask yourself: Is the person leaning toward you away from you, or is there a great deal of space between you? Is the person sitting upright or slumping?

- Examine facial expressions. Human beings can understand a great deal about each other by watching facial expressions. Notice: Is the person smiling, eye-rolling, grimacing, or frowning? Does the person look animated, blank, or angry?

- Observe gestures. People often provide information about their state of mind by making gestures. Pay attention and ask yourself: Is the person pointing, clenching fists, pacing, rubbing the back of his or her neck, throwing things, pounding fists on the table, punching walls, hugging you, holding your hand, or slamming doors? If the person is pounding his fists or punching walls, you can assume that he is angry or frustrated. If he is smiling or hugging you warmly, you can assume that he is feeling warm and friendly.

Capturing Feelings—Empathically listening to the emotional content of the message.

- Decode the verbal message by listening to the feelings being expressed beneath the content itself.

- What is the other person feeling?

- How might this situation bring up memories from this person's past?

- Are there elements in this person's family history that can help me understand his or her feelings on a deeper level?

- Am I noticing recurring themes in the messages sent that can give me clues to what the person is feeling?

- Is there an added intensity to the person's feelings because of factors I might not yet know about or understand?

SKILL 2: SENDING

Sending Spoken Messages—Conveying information in a clear, nonthreatening, and respectful way.

- Communicate your message by using I-statements. I-statements are a way to talk about problems in a relationship without attacking the other person. I-statements allow you to take responsibility for the message you're sending, express your feelings, and focus on the behavior that's bothering you. Consider the difference between these two statements:

    1) "I sometimes feel sad and miss you when the one evening off a week we have is spent playing pool";

2) **Attacking** "You're inconsiderate. You always leave me at home while you're out playing pool with your buddies!"

- Remember that it's okay to have an opinion and to express it with clarity and respect.

- Stick to the main topic. Don't meander or add extraneous subjects to the conversation. Stay in the present; don't focus on the past.

- Be reasonably concise. Stay away from compound sentences—no ranting. Don't spend many hours belaboring your point.

- Solicit feedback in order to clarify that your message is being understood. Show the listener that his or her viewpoint matters to you.

- Maintain a conversational tone while sending your message.

- Refrain from using the words should, ought, and must.

- Be willing to generate options and solutions when resolving a dispute.

Sending Nonverbal Messages—Conveying your message so that it will be received.

- Convey your message at a conversational volume, with open body posture, agreeable facial expressions, and appropriate gestures.

- Refrain from screaming, yelling, or escalated volume.

- Maintain an open body posture by facing the person you're talking to, not folding your arms, not crossing your legs, and by sitting upright.

- Don't roll your eyes.

- Don't frown, grimace, or furrow your brow.

- Don't use threatening gestures, such as pointing, fist-clenching, door-slamming, or getting in someone's face.

Sending Feelings—Conveying the emotional content of your message in an open, honest, sensitive manner. Be in touch with your feelings.

- Take some time to explore your feelings and determine what the primary feeling is.

- Be clear and honest about your feelings—own up to what you're feeling without blaming, accusing, or attacking.

- Be aware of past issues that might be coming up and complicating your ability to see the current situation clearly. Take responsibility for your own baggage.

- Show empathy for the listener while expressing your own feelings. Be willing to compromise.

- Ask yourself, "Is the intensity of my feeling appropriate to the situation?"

CONFLICT RESOLUTION

When two people are in conflict, it comes as no surprise that tempers can flare and anger can dominate. We have all had the experience of starting a conversation that turns into a disagreement, then an argument, and perhaps eventually a full-blown fight. By learning a few simple steps, you can approach problematic subjects more gently, hold respectful conversations about those subjects, and resolve conflict successfully. Read through the chart in Exercise 18 and become familiar with the suggestions. Next time you find yourself in conflict with your partner, review this chart and work through the steps. I bet you'll be pleasantly surprised.

EXERCISE 18: YOUR CONFLICT RESOLUTION

Choose a recurring conflict to work through with your partner to bring old issues to resolution. Make sure you work on the conflict-resolution steps when neither of you are angry. Focus on choosing a specific area of the conflict to work through. It might take you multiple attempts to process and negotiate through all areas of a conflict.

Focus on collaboration, not on winning. Try to stay within a 45-minute time frame. If you go over that time frame, take a break. Come back to the negotiation at an agreed-upon time in the future. Remember that this strategy will take practice! See the ***Jumpstart Exercise to help you complete this exercise.***

1. Pinpoint the conflict.

   a) Start by saying something positive about the problem.

   b) Be precise about the conflict.

   c) Communicate your feelings with the use of "I feel" statements. Start with "I feel (emotion) when (behavior) happens." Stay away from "you," "always," and "never" statements.

   d) Approach the problem in as few sentences as possible with an attitude of teamwork. Stay away from compound sentences and root cause analysis. Avoid the "Why" questions and focus on the "What" and the "How."

   e) Each person needs to be accountable for his or her own role in the conflict.

f) Stay on topic. Don't focus on past experiences.

g) Make sure you understand by listening without interrupting, assuming, or inferring.

h) Restate what you have heard to confirm that you understand and to show that you're listening. Ask for clarification if you don't understand.

i) Show empathy by imagining how the other person might be feeling. Consider how that person might perceive the issue.

j) Avoid sarcasm and blame.

k) If the other person becomes defensive, this is your cue to step back and listen. If you feel defensive, admit it.

2. Generate a list of possible solutions.

3. Explore the solutions.
   a) As you process the list together, look for mutually beneficial solutions.
   b) Discuss the pros and cons of each possible solution.

4. Choose a solution and test it for 1–2 weeks.

5. Reconvene to evaluate whether your solution solved the problem. If not, then choose another solution from your list, and follow steps 4 and 5 again.

Jumpstart the Exercise: Ellen's Example

1. Pinpoint the conflict.

    a) Start by saying something positive about the problem.

    Positive Example: "I really enjoy it when you include me in discussion about our finances, but sometimes I feel overwhelmed by our talks."

    Negative Example: "Why do you always keep me in discussions about money that last forever?"

    b) Be precise about the conflict.

    Focus on one aspect of the problem and resolve it. For instance, focus on the fact that you have trouble engaging in a conversation about money when you expect that the discussion will last many hours.

    Precise Declaration: "It's not that I don't want to have the conversations at all; I just feel overwhelmed by the length of the discussions."

    c) Communicate your feelings with the use of "I feel" statements. Start with "I feel (emotion) when (behavior) happens." Stay away from "you," "always," and "never" statements.

    *Example: "I feel **overwhelmed** when our discussions last more than 45 minutes."*

    d) Approach the problem in as few sentences as possible with an attitude of teamwork. Stay away from compound sentences and root cause analysis. Avoid the "Why" questions and focus on the "What" and the "How."

    Positive Example: "We seem to have long discussions when we talk about money. I tend to feel overwhelmed. I wonder if we could set up an agreed-upon time frame for our money discussions."

    Negative Example: "Why do you always go on and on every time you talk about money? You're just like your stingy mother—she pinches every penny. Why can't you just leave me alone and stop trying to change the way I handle money?"

    e) Each person needs to be accountable for his or her own role in the conflict.

    Example: "I'm sorry that I tend to spend so much time on conversations about money and that it causes you to feel overwhelmed."

    "I'm sorry I get so flooded when we talk about money and it makes you feel like I don't care."

    f) Stay on topic. Don't focus on past experiences.

    Example: "Let's talk about what happened this morning in the car on the way to the bank—I promise not to bring up subjects from the past."

    g) Make sure you understand by listening without interrupting, assuming, or inferring.

    Example: "I want to make sure I'm hearing you right—so please finish what you're saying. I'll tell you my perspective once I can be sure I've understood your side."

    h) Restate what you have heard to confirm that you understand and to show that you're listening. Ask for clarification if you don't understand.

    Example: "I think what I'm hearing is that you want to know more about our financial situation, and you want to talk about it for a reasonably short period of time. Am I getting it right?"

    i) Show empathy by imagining how the other person might be feeling. Consider how that person might perceive the issue.

Example: "I imagine that you sometimes feel in the dark about our finances, and that probably scares you. Once we do start talking about money, you probably want to keep talking about it because you're not sure when I'll open up about it again."

j) Avoid sarcasm and blame.

Example: DO NOT say, "Your parents are both terrible with money. Why don't you just let me handle it and stop trying to be the 'Online Banking Queen'?"

k) If the other person becomes defensive, this is your cue to step back and listen. If you feel defensive, admit it.

Example: "I can see that you're feeling defensive, and I can understand why. Let me step back and try to listen more carefully, okay?"—and "I'm starting to feel defensive, and I know that's making this conversation more difficult. Let me press my mental 'reset' button and we can try again."

2. Generate a list of possible solutions.

- *Let's write out our ideas about how we each think money should be spent and then compare notes.*
- *Let's set a rule that our conversations about money will not last more than 45 minutes.*
- *Maybe we can talk about the pros and cons of having joint bank accounts.*
- *I can commit to not avoiding the topic of money, and you can commit to not overfocusing on the topic to the exclusion of other important subjects.*

3. Explore the solutions.

a) As you process the list together, look for mutually beneficial solutions.

b) Discuss the pros and cons of each possible solution.

4. Choose a solution and test it for 1–2 weeks.

5. Reconvene to evaluate whether your solution solved the problem. If not, then choose another solution from your list, and follow steps 4 and 5 again.

DEALING WITH DIFFERENCES

All relationships have differences. At an early age, you can begin to detect differences in personality, communication, and coping abilities within your family. In a close relationship, it is inevitable that you will encounter differences between yourself and your partner. Even though you might see eye to eye on many subjects, you still discover areas of dissimilarity. Differences in traits, perspectives, or style can create conflict.

EXERCISE 19: DEALING WITH DIFFERENCES

This exercise asks you to take an inventory of some of the major differences between you and your partner. Once you have highlighted those differences, the exercise helps you explore ways to understand, accept, and value those differences. See the *Jumpstart Exercise to help you complete this exercise.*

1.   Take an inventory of your own traits by circling the qualities that apply to you.

COMMUNICATION TRAITS

Overcommunicator	Undercommunicator
Harsh	Sensitive
Loud	Soft
Passive	Aggressive
Fast	Slow
Direct	Avoidant

Name some of your own:

SEXUAL TRAITS

High libido	Low libido
Adventurous	Traditional
Open	Closed
Communicative	Noncommunicative
High frequency	Low frequency

Name some of your own:

FINANCIAL TRAITS

Spender	Frugal
Conceals purchases	Open about purchases
Controlling about money	Laid back about money
Good money manager	Poor money manager
Future-oriented/Invests	Present-oriented/Lives for today

Name some of your own:

FAMILY OF ORIGIN TRAITS

Enmeshed	Independent
Controlling	Relaxed
Affectionate	Standoffish
Angry	Happy
Nosy	Disinterested
Stable	Unstable

Name some of your own:

2. Have your partner examine their traits by circling the qualities that apply.

COMMUNICATION TRAITS

Overcommunicator	Undercommunicator
Harsh	Sensitive
Loud	Soft
Passive	Aggressive
Fast	Slow
Direct	Avoidant

Name some of your own:

SEXUAL TRAITS

High libido	Low libido
Adventurous	Traditional
Open	Closed
Communicative	Noncommunicative
High frequency	Low frequency

Name some of your own:

FINANCIAL TRAITS

Spender	Frugal
Conceals purchases	Open about purchases
Controlling about money	Laid back about money
Good money manager	Poor money manager
Future-oriented/Invests	Present-oriented/Lives for today

Name some of your own:

FAMILY OF ORIGIN TRAITS

Enmeshed	Independent
Controlling	Relaxed
Affectionate	Standoffish
Angry	Happy
Nosy	Disinterested
Stable	Unstable

Name some of your own:

3. Ask yourself if there are some ways you can begin to appreciate and value the differences between you and your partner identified in Step 2. Look at the contrasts and try to understand how those differences balance you as a couple.

CONTRASTING COMMUNICATION TRAITS

MY TRAIT	MY PARTNER'S TRAIT

a) How does this difference show up in my relationship?

b) How could this difference help us as a couple?

c) How can I better accept this difference between us?

CONTRASTING SEXUAL TRAITS

MY TRAIT	MY PARTNER'S TRAIT

a) How does this difference show up in my relationship?

b) How could this difference help us as a couple?

c) How can I better accept this difference between us?

CONTRASTING FINANCIAL TRAITS

MY TRAIT	MY PARTNER'S TRAIT

a) How does this difference show up in my relationship?

b) How could this difference help us as a couple?

c) How can I better accept this difference between us?

CONTRASTING FAMILY OF ORIGIN TRAITS

MY TRAIT	MY PARTNER'S TRAIT

a) How does this difference show up in my relationship?

b) How could this difference help us as a couple?

c) How can I better accept this difference between us?

Jumpstart the Exercise: Bob's Example

1. Take an inventory of your own traits by circling the qualities that apply to you.

COMMUNICATION TRAITS

Overcommunicator	Undercommunicator
Harsh	Sensitive
Loud	Soft
Passive	**Aggressive**
Fast	Slow
Direct	Avoidant

Name some of your own: *Threatening, Intimidating, Willing to work on it*

SEXUAL TRAITS

High libido	Low libido
Adventurous	Traditional
Open	Closed
Communicative	Noncommunicative
High frequency	Low frequency

Name some of your own: *Ties sex to self-worth, Initiates sex*

FINANCIAL TRAITS

Spender	**Frugal**
Conceals purchases	Open about purchases
Controlling about money	Laid back about money
Good money manager	Poor money manager
Future-oriented/Invests	Present-oriented/Lives for today

Name some of your own: *Nervous about becoming poor, Conscientious about spending*

FAMILY OF ORIGIN TRAITS

Enmeshed	**Independent**
Controlling	Relaxed
Affectionate	**Standoffish**
Angry	Happy
Nosy	**Disinterested**
Stable	**Unstable**

Name some of your own: *Selfish*

2. Have your partner examine their traits by circling the qualities that apply.

Overcommunicator	Undercommunicator
Harsh	**Sensitive**
Loud	**Soft**
Passive	Aggressive
Fast	Slow
Direct	Avoidant

Name some of your own: *Considerate*

SEXUAL TRAITS

High libido	**Low libido**
Adventurous	**Traditional**
Open	Closed
Communicative	Noncommunicative
High frequency	**Low frequency**

Name some of your own: *Almost never initiates sex*

FINANCIAL TRAITS

Spender	Frugal
Conceals purchases	**Open about purchases**
Controlling about money	**Laid back about money**
Good money manager	Poor money manager
Future-oriented/Invests	**Present-oriented/Lives for today**

Name some of your own: *Not fearful about poverty*

FAMILY OF ORIGIN TRAITS

Enmeshed	Independent
Controlling	Relaxed
Affectionate	Standoffish
Angry	**Happy**
Nosy	Disinterested
Stable	Unstable

Name some of your own: *Active/energetic, Close*

3. Ask yourself if there are some ways you can begin to appreciate and value the differences between you and your partner identified in Step 2. Look at the contrasts and try to understand how those differences balance you as a couple.

CONTRASTING COMMUNICATION TRAITS

MY TRAIT	MY PARTNER'S TRAIT
Agressive	*Soft and Sensitive*

a) How does this difference show up in my relationship?

It shows up mostly when I'm being pushy. It's amazing to see how nicely she approaches me when she has a problem, but I seem to do the opposite. I attack first and apologize later.

b) How could this difference help us as a couple?

This difference can help us as a couple as I learn from her softer way of communicating. She is teaching me that you don't have to shout to be heard.

c) How can I better accept this difference between us?

I hope it helps her allow for imperfection in me while I take time to improve this part of myself. I am glad we're different in this way because I need her help when it comes to learning how to soften my approach.

CONTRASTING SEXUAL TRAITS

MY TRAIT	MY PARTNER'S TRAIT
High libido	*Low libido*

a) How does this difference show up in my relationship?

I often want sex when my partner isn't in the mood.

b) How could this difference help us as a couple?

Well, I'm not sure. I guess it makes me value the experience more when we do finally have sex. I think it makes her feel very desired, since I'm always willing to have sex. I never say no.

c) How can I better accept this difference between us?

I do value the fact that even infrequent sex is meaningful to her and that she enjoys it. I'm trying to learn how to see that everyone has a different level of sex drive and that there is no right or wrong amount of frequency of sex in a relationship. I want her to feel loved and desired, not criticized and judged.

CONTRASTING FINANCIAL TRAITS

MY TRAIT	MY PARTNER'S TRAIT
Frugal	*Spender*

a) How does this difference show up in my relationship?

It shows up in my occasional freak-outs about whether we have enough money to go on vacation to-gether. It shows up when I try to tell her how to spend her money.

b) How could this difference help us as a couple?

She might be able to teach me how to relax about money, and I might be able to teach her how to show more discipline in this area.

c) How can I better accept this difference between us?

I want to be able to appreciate my girlfriend's sense of financial freedom—she seems so easygoing and so unafraid about money. I like that about her, and I wish I could be that way. I hope she values the fact that I want to provide for us both in the future, and that it matters to me that I can take care of her.

CONTRASTING FAMILY OF ORIGIN TRAITS

MY TRAIT	MY PARTNER'S TRAIT
Standoffish	*Affectionate*

a) How does this difference show up in my relationship?

Sometimes I forget to kiss my girlfriend hello and goodbye. Sometimes I'm not as affectionate with her as she wants me to be when were in public. She gets upset when I don't hold her hand or sit next to her.

b) How could this difference help us as a couple?

It already helps me a great deal. I feel loved by her, and I'm learning to be more affectionate in ways that don't always have to lead to sex. I'm especially proud that she wants me to kiss her hello and good-bye. I'm getting better about remembering to do it.

c) How can I better accept this difference between us?

My partner has made room for me to be a little more to myself sometimes. Other times she lets me know what she needs in a sweet and loving way. I don't mind this difference between us, but I think she does. I'm trying to close the gap a little bit more when it comes to this difference. I like that she doesn't require for me to be exactly like she is in regard to affection.

FAIR FIGHTING CONTRACT

Anger triggers lead to angry episodes unless you have agreements in place to re-route the conflict toward a more constructive collaboration. The Fair Fighting Contract helps couples commit to reasonable and respectful behavior during arguments. During fights, people tend to play one of two roles. One person wants to resolve the issue and the other person wants to retreat. People sometimes switch roles as well.

The Fair Fighting Contract is designed to help couples use time away to prevent anger from escalating and conflicts from remaining unresolved. The rules for completing the contract are as follows:

✓ Speak for yourself, not for your partner.

✓ Stay away from judging your partner's responses.

✓ Don't interrupt.

EXERCISE 20: YOUR FAIR FIGHTING CONTRACT

Collaborate with your partner to complete the contract below: See the *Jumpstart Exercise to help you complete this exercise.*

1. Know your anger cues. I will know that my anger is rising by observing these cues:

	PARTNER 1	PARTNER 2
Thoughts		
Feelings		
Behaviors		

2. Agree on a "time-out" signal and statement. If I exhibit any of the above anger cues, I agree to use a "Rest Period" Signal and Statement.

PARTNER 1	PARTNER 2
My "Rest Period" Signal and Statement will be:	
Commit to not sabotaging the "Rest Period":	
• I will not hassle or pursue my partner when he or she calls for a Rest Period. • I will not drive. • I will not drink alcohol or do drugs. • I will not gossip with other people about the dispute. • I will not stew and/or work myself back up into an angrier state. • I will not focus on resentments. • I will not hit, kick, door-slam, wall-punch, or exhibit any physical violence. • I will not say things under my breath as I exit the situation. • I will not threaten suicide.	• I will not hassle or pursue my partner when he or she calls for a Rest Period. • I will not drive. • I will not drink alcohol or do drugs. • I will not gossip with other people about the dispute. • I will not stew and/or work myself back up into an angrier state. • I will not focus on resentments. • I will not hit, kick, door-slam, wall-punch, or exhibit any physical violence. • I will not say things under my breath as I exit the situation. • I will not threaten suicide.

3. Commit to where, when, and how.

PARTNER 1	PARTNER 2
When I take my "Rest Period," here is where I will go <u>during</u> the break and here is where I will return <u>after</u> the break:	
When I take my "Rest Period," here is where I will NOT go:	
When I take a Rest Period, it will last this long:	
Here's HOW I will use the Rest Period to de-escalate anger and resolve the problem: Place a check-mark next to the strategies you plan to use during your Rest Period:	
☐ *Deep breathing exercises* ☐ *Physical exercise* ☐ *Brainstorm solutions to resolve the problem* ☐ *Consider your partner's perspective* ☐ *Acknowledge your own role in the conflict* ☐ *Clarify your own needs* ☐ *Examine your own coping strategies* ☐ *Focus on the good intentions on both sides* ☐ *Remember that it's ok to have differences of opinion* ☐ *Use affirmations and visualization to calm your anger* ☐ *I commit to returning to the conversation immediately after this time period has passed* ☐ *Generate some of your own:*	☐ *Deep breathing exercises* ☐ *Physical exercise* ☐ *Brainstorm solutions to resolve the problem* ☐ *Consider your partner's perspective* ☐ *Acknowledge your own role in the conflict* ☐ *Clarify your own needs* ☐ *Examine your own coping strategies* ☐ *Focus on the good intentions on both sides* ☐ *Remember that it's ok to have differences of opinion* ☐ *Use affirmations and visualization to calm your anger* ☐ *I commit to returning to the conversation immediately after this time period has passed* ☐ *Generate some of your own:*

4. Coming back.

Here is what I will do once the Rest Period is over:

- Talk calmly about my own feelings and perceptions.

- Own up to my own role in the conflict.

- Avoid blaming, accusing, berating my partner.

- Maintain a conversational tone.

- Keep an open body posture.

- Be willing to collaborate and come to a resolution.

I am signing this contract as a commitment to collaborate and resolve conflict in a healthy manner.

Signed:_____Date:_____

Signed: _____Date:_____

Jumpstart the Exercise: Bob and Sue's Example

1. Know your anger cues. I will know that my anger is rising by observing these cues:

	PARTNER 1	PARTNER 2
Thoughts	*"How DARE you?"* *"This isn't FAIR!"* *"You don't even care about me!"*	*"Here we go again!"* *"It's always something."* *"Why does this always happen?"*
Feelings	*Jealousy* *Fear* *Frustration*	*Exasperation* *Frustration* *Anxiety*
Behaviors	*Raising my voice* *Clenching my fists and/or my jaw* *Pacing* *Name-calling*	*Shrugging my shoulders* *Eye-rolling* *Grimacing* *Door-slamming*

2. Agree on a "time-out" signal and statement.

PARTNER 1	PARTNER 2
If I exhibit any of the above anger cues, I agree to use a "Rest Period" Signal and Statement. My "Rest Period" Signal and Statement will be:	
I will use the "T" for Time-Out Signal, and I can say, "I need a break."	*I'll agree to use the "T" for Time-Out Signal, too, and I'll say, "I need a break."*
Commit to not sabotaging the "Rest Period":	
• *I will not hassle or pursue my partner when he or she calls for a Rest Period.* • *I will not drive.* • *I will not drink alcohol or do drugs.* • *I will not gossip with other people about the dispute.* • *I will not stew and/or work myself back up into an angrier state.* • *I will not focus on resentments.* • *I will not hit, kick, door-slam, wall-punch, or exhibit any physical violence.* • *I will not say things under my breath as I exit the situation.* • *I will not threaten suicide.*	• *I will not hassle or pursue my partner when he or she calls for a Rest Period.* • *I will not drive.* • *I will not drink alcohol or do drugs.* • *I will not gossip with other people about the dispute.* • *I will not stew and/or work myself back up into an angrier state.* • *I will not focus on resentments.* • *I will not hit, kick, door-slam, wall-punch, or exhibit any physical violence.* • *I will not say things under my breath as I exit the situation.* • *I will not threaten suicide.*

3. Commit to where, when, and how.

PARTNER 1	PARTNER 2
When I take my "Rest Period," here is where I will go during the break and here is where I will return after the break:	
I will go to my home office during the break. *I will return to the living room after the break.*	*I will go to the exercise room or the garden during the break.* *I will return to the living room after the break.*
When I take my "Rest Period," here is where I will NOT go:	
The kitchen (unless I need to grab a sandwich, but I'll leave immediately after that).	*The kitchen*
When I take a Rest Period, it will last this long:	
45 minutes	45 minutes
Here's how I will use the Rest Period to de-escalate anger and resolve the problem: Place a check-mark next to the strategies you plan to use during your Rest Period:	
• Deep breathing exercises • Physical exercise • Brainstorm solutions to resolve the problem. • Consider your partner's perspective. • Acknowledge your own role in the conflict. • Clarify your own needs. • Examine your own coping strategies. • Focus on the good intentions on both sides. • Remember that it's okay to have differences of opinion. • Use affirmations and visualization to calm your anger. • I commit to returning to the conversation immediately after this time period has passed. • Generate some of your own: • *Remember how much she loves me* • *Do a project* • *Listen to calming music*	• Deep breathing exercises • Physical exercise • Brainstorm solutions to resolve the problem. • Consider your partner's perspective. • Acknowledge your own role in the conflict. • Clarify your own needs. • Examine your own coping strategies. • Focus on the good intentions on both sides. • Remember that it's okay to have differences of opinion. • Use affirmations and visualization to calm your anger. • I commit to returning to the conversation immediately after this time period has passed. • Generate some of your own: • *Visualize our wedding* • *Think about Bob's good traits* • *Remind myself that this will pass* • *Write in my journal*

4. Coming Back.

Here is what I will do once the Rest Period is over:

- Talk calmly about my own feelings and perceptions.

- Own up to my own role in the conflict.

- Avoid blaming, accusing, berating my partner.

- Maintain a conversational tone.

- Keep an open body posture.

- Be willing to collaborate and come to a resolution.

I am signing this contract as a commitment to collaborate and resolve conflict in a healthy manner.

Signed: _Robert William Everyman_   Date: _January 1, 2012_

Signed: _Sue Katherine Everywoman_   Date: _January 1, 2012_

HOW ENVIRONMENT AFFECTS ANGER

Humans are creatures of habit. We learn behavioral patterns based on our past experiences. Our environment provides triggers that can activate defensive postures, negative patterns, and unconstructive behaviors. For instance, if you normally have disagreements in the kitchen, you establish an association between arguments and the kitchen, making the kitchen a potential place of conflict.

EXERCISE 21: ENVIRONMENTAL TRIGGERS

This exercise helps you identify the environmental triggers that create conflict. Once you have become aware of your environmental triggers, you can begin to establish new patterns. See the ***Jumpstart Exercise to help you complete this exercise.***

1. Where do you primarily have conflict? For instance, do you have a "This is where we fight" room? (kitchen, bathroom, bedroom, living room, etc.)

2. Are there places in the home where you tend to go to "cool off"?

3. Are there areas in the home that you consider to be more "Your Space/Turf"?

4. Are there areas in the home that you consider to be more "My Partner's Space/Turf"?

5. Are there spaces in the home that are considered to be "Shared Space"?

TO ESTABLISH NEW PATTERNS WE WILL FOLLOW A THREE-STEP PROCESS:

1. Agree on a neutral space.

Talk to your partner and agree on a neutral space. Now identify your neutral space:
- ☐ Kitchen
- ☐ Living room
- ☐ Den
- ☐ Bathroom
- ☐ Formal dining room
- ☐ Game/Media room
- ☐ Front porch
- ☐ Back patio
- ☐ Guest-house
- ☐ Office
- ☐ Workout room
- ☐ Other:

2. Become aware.

When conflict arises, become aware of *where* you are arguing. Ask yourself:

- "Is this a 'where we fight' room?" ☐ Yes ☐ No

- "Are we on 'my turf' or 'my partner's turf'?" ☐ Yes ☐ No

- More thoughts:

3. Change location.

Respectfully request to change your location and move to a neutral space in order to resolve the conflict more effectively.

SUGGESTIONS FOR MAKING THE REQUEST:

- "I feel like we're not going to be fair to this conversation; can we move this discussion to _____ (neutral space)?"

- "It seems like we tend to argue more heatedly in the _____ (fight zone), but we have more constructive conversations in the _____ (neutral space). I want to make sure we resolve this conflict. Can we move to the _____ (neutral space)?"

- "If you think we might need a break, we could hold off on this discussion for now and reconvene in the _____ (neutral space) in 30 minutes."

- Generate your own:

1. Where do you primarily have conflict? For instance, do you have a "This is where we fight" room? (kitchen, bathroom, bedroom, living room, etc.)

    Yes, my wife and I tend to fight in the kitchen.

2. Are there places in the home where you tend to go to "cool off"?

    I go to the office, and she goes to the exercise room.

3. Are there areas in the home that you consider to be more "Your Space/Turf"?

    Yes, the office is my turf.

4. Are there areas in the home that you consider to be more "My Partner's Space/Turf"?

    Yes, the garden and exercise room are her turf.

5. Are there spaces in the home that are considered to be "Shared Space"?

    Yes, the living room, the den, and the dining room.

TO ESTABLISH NEW PATTERNS, WE WILL FOLLOW A THREE-STEP PROCESS:

1. Agree on a neutral space. Talk to your partner and agree on a neutral space. Now identify your neutral space: *the den.*

2. Become aware.

When conflict arises, become aware of *where* you are arguing. Ask yourself:

- "Is this a 'where we fight' room?" ☑ Yes   ☐ No

- "Are we on 'my turf' or 'my partner's turf'?" ☐ Yes   ☑ No

- More thoughts:
  More thoughts: The other day as I realized my wife and I were beginning to argue, I also noticed that we were in the kitchen. We weren't on either person's "turf," but we WERE in our "This is Where We Fight" room.

3. Change location.

    Respectfully request to change your location and move to a neutral space in order to resolve the conflict more effectively.

SUGGESTIONS FOR MAKING THE REQUEST:

- "I feel like we're not going to be fair to this conversation. Can we move this discussion to *the den* (neutral space)?"

- "It seems like we tend to argue more heatedly in the *kitchen* (fight zone), but we have more constructive conversations in the *den* (neutral space). I want to make sure we resolve this conflict. Can we move to the *den* (neutral space)?"

- "If you think we might need a break, we could hold off on this discussion for now and reconvene in the *den* (neutral space) in 30 minutes."

- Generate your own:

    "Honey, I really want to hear you fully and resolve this disagreement. I think we'll have a better chance of doing that if we move to a more neutral space, like the den. Our fights tend to escalate when we're in the kitchen, and I want to make sure we talk this out calmly."

◈ SACRED SPACES WHERE FIGHTING IS ALWAYS OFF-LIMITS

Many people wait until the end of the day to start intense discussions, bringing conflict directly into the bedroom at nighttime. This can impact sleep and relaxation, because you and your partner might both become tense and upset precisely when sleep is most needed.

Repeatedly starting arguments in the bedroom can create an unsafe environment for sleep and sex. If you create a correlation between the bedroom and conflict, this correlation can seriously damage intimacy rather than creating it.

Have a conversation with your partner about maintaining your bedroom as a sacred space. If an argument arises, agree to move to a neutral space.

CHAPTER FOUR

Setting Boundaries

My client Rachel has been dating a nice guy named Eric. On their first date, she overdisclosed, confiding how "broken" she is, how much anguish she feels over her brother's alcoholism, how no one has ever loved her unconditionally. She doesn't know how to pace getting to know someone, going gradually as intimacy grows. Within days, Rachel was buying Eric expensive gifts and treating him to elaborate restaurants. No matter what Eric says he wants, Rachel obliges, and why not? She has no boundaries.

Without boundaries, it is difficult to feel safe, define your identity, speak with conviction, or organize your life. But just what is a boundary? I can tell you what is *not* a boundary: It's not a 12-foot-high brick wall or a line in the sand. A boundary is a clear sense of where you end and another person begins. It's an invisible force field that keeps your mind, heart, and soul from leaking out all over another person, to the detriment of your own integrity.

Boundaries create structure, peace, safety, communication, and strong relationships in our lives. They are a basic ingredient for a healthy, happy life, offering the following benefits:

✓ Boundaries help define your sense of self—they provide you with borders, helping you know where you start and where the other person begins.

✓ Boundaries keep you safe from harm—they protect you from destructive people, harmful situations, and damaging beliefs.

✓ Boundaries enable you to speak for yourself—they allow you to maintain an inner and outer sense of conviction about what and how you communicate your needs, wants, opinions, and feelings.

✓ Boundaries convey strength and confidence—they attract healthy people who are interested in positive growth.

✓ Boundaries help to organize your life—they bring order to your schedule, your plans, your obligations, and your activities.

Boundaries help you decide what you want to be within your life, what you want to have within your life, whom you want to welcome into your life, and how you want to structure your life.

Growing up, for better or for worse, we learn how to set and communicate boundaries by watching the way our family members respond to each other. As we absorb and imitate their patterns, our future boundary-setting skills begin to take shape. See the **Jumpstart Exercise to help you complete this exercise.**

EXERCISE 22: YOUR BOUNDARY HISTORY

1. What did you witness about your parents' ability to say no and set limits with family members?

2. Do you feel uncomfortable saying "No"?

3. Are you a people pleaser?

4. If so, how does being a pleaser affect the way you demonstrate your anger?

5. Do you have people in your life who are placing undue expectations on you in regard to physical space, time, and emotional involvement?

6. Are you able or unable to set limits with them?

7. Was your family overinvolved with each other?

8. How much time do you spend with others socially or interpersonally on a daily basis?

9. Do you wish you had more time or less with certain people?

10. How much solitude or "alone time" do you get in your daily life? Is it enough? Too much?

11. Do you find yourself isolating? (Isolating means that you separate yourself from other people, spend time alone because you fear being too close to people, or seek an excessive amount of privacy.)

12. How important is connectedness to you?

13. Did you get much privacy in your family?

14. How much personal information do you feel comfortable offering to strangers, friends, and family members?

15. Do you say too much or "overdisclose" on a first meeting?

16. Do you find yourself withholding information from strangers, friends, and family members?

17. Is privacy important to you?

18. Were your parents physically or emotionally available to you?

19. Do you feel uncomfortable asking for more love, time, affection, or help from people in your life?

20. Do you tend to spend a lot of time alone? If so, do you think it affects how you express anger?

21. Were your parents rigid and controlling with family members?

22. When your boundaries have been violated, do you become resentful, passive-aggressive, and/or explosive in your anger?

23. Do you suspect you might need to show more respect for the boundaries of others? How so?

24. Do you see any similarities between the way you set boundaries now and the way your family established boundaries?

25. Which areas of your life (work, family, friendships, intimate relationships, etc.) are most affected by the way you handle boundaries and the way you handle anger?

Jumpstart the Exercise: Bob's Example

1. What did you witness about your parents' ability to say no and set limits with family members?

   My stepdad said "No" a lot, but my mom and my sister never listened. They ignored him.

2. Do you feel uncomfortable saying "No"?

   Not really. I feel like I tell people "no" a lot.

3. Are you a people pleaser?

   No. I really don't care what most people think. I probably only care about what my girlfriend thinks.

4. If so, how does being a pleaser affect the way you demonstrate your anger?

   I don't care that much about pleasing people, and I set VERY strong boundaries.

5. Do you have people in your life who are placing undue expectations on you in regard to physical space, time, and emotional involvement? For instance, do you have friends who expect you to be available to them constantly, family members who pressure you to give them money, or co-workers who seek an excessive amount of closeness?

   I'm not sure. Sometimes I wish I could set better limits about how much I work. Other than that, I don't really let people put too many expectations on me. I put expectations on myself.

6. Are you able or unable to set limits with them?

   If people push me, I set limits by making a scene or by leaving entirely.

7. Was your family overinvolved with each other?

   My family was not really involved with each other's lives. No one really related to anyone else. Everyone just did whatever they wanted to do, on their own, mostly.

8. How much time do you spend with others socially or interpersonally on a daily basis?

   Other than work, I spend a lot of time alone.

9. Do you wish you had more time or less with certain people?

   I wish I had more time with my girlfriend and less time at my job.

10. How much solitude or "alone time" do you get in your daily life? Is it enough? Too much?

    I get plenty of alone time, maybe too much.

11. Do you find yourself isolating?

    Maybe sometimes.

12. How important is connectedness to you?

    It's pretty important to me—especially with my girlfriend.

13. Did you get much privacy in your family?

    Privacy wasn't a problem because we all led such separate lives. We didn't even eat dinner together. I don't remember my mom ever asking me a personal question or even coming into my bedroom.

14. How much personal information do you feel comfortable offering to strangers, friends, and family members?

    I'm a very, very private person. I don't like to tell people my business.

15. Do you say too much or "overdisclose" on a first meeting?

    I don't talk much when I first meet people.

16. Do you find yourself withholding information from strangers, friends, and family members?

    I don't generally tell people a lot of my business because I don't trust people.

17. Is privacy important to you?

    Yes, very important.

18. Were your parents physically or emotionally available to you?

    My stepdad never really talked to me or hugged me. My mom would talk a lot but not really about much that had anything to do with me.

19. Do you feel uncomfortable asking for more love, time, affection, or help from people in your life?

    Yes, I feel uncomfortable—I almost never ask for more of anything.

20. Do you tend to spend a lot of time alone? If so, do you think it affects how you express anger?

    I do spend a lot of time alone. Yes, it usually makes me angrier—I stew.

21. Were your parents rigid and controlling with family members?

    My stepdad tried to control my life a lot, but it never worked.

22. When your boundaries have been violated, do you become resentful, passive agressive, and/or explosive in your anger?

    I become resentful and explosive in my anger.

23. Do you suspect you might need to show more respect for the boundaries of others? How so?

    Yes, I think that I probably need to show more respect for other people. I sometimes forget to ask what other people need or want because I'm so busy trying to make sure I get my own needs met. I need to slow down and remember that other people matter too.

24. Do you see any similarities between the way you set boundaries now and the way your family established boundaries?

    Yes, I can see both sides. I sometimes set strong boundaries around privacy—like my stepdad did when he would retreat to the garage. And yet sometimes I lose control by ranting and raving like my mom and my sister, and I steamroll over other people's boundaries when I do that.

25. Which areas of your life (work, family, friendships, intimate relationships, etc.) are most affected by the way you handle boundaries and the way you handle anger?

    My relationship with my girlfriend is most affected by the way I handle boundaries.

BETTER BOUNDARIES

Just as having appropriate boundaries contributes to healthy relationships, having trouble with boundaries will cause problems in relationships. If you've discovered you lack certain boundaries, you can gradually learn to establish them. But it's impossible to set a boundary unless you know exactly who *you* are: and most of us have given barely a thought to this essential idea.

Many people's "self-concept"—who they believe they are—is based on external factors such as looks, money, career, house, car, relationships, awards, and clothes. You might believe, "If my partner loves me and thinks I am attractive, then I am lovable." If we tie our self-concept to external factors, it will fluctuate up and down based on these external factors. This instability can affect the way we handle our emotions, especially anger. How we manage anger directly correlates with how we view ourselves.

If you tie your self-worth to your career, for example, you might lose a job and then your self-image will plummet. The worse you feel about yourself, the more irritable you become at home. You might begin taking your anger out on a partner or spouse.

I witnessed that scenario firsthand with a client. A couple, who had been married two years, was having terrible fights. The wife claimed it was because her husband wasn't helping enough with their baby. But as we delved deeper, it became clear that her anger was rooted in the fact that she had given up working—at her husband's request. She had run her own very successful company as a literary agent, and being "just" a stay-at-home mom made her feel worthless. Her husband was the closest target for her irritability and resentment.

You can see how such a self-concept is not conducive to managing anger well. The more stable and secure your self-concept is, the better able you will be to tame your temper.

Self-concept rests on three legs: identity, acceptance, and confidence. Here is how I define them:

1. *Identity:* a sense of who you are and of what characterizes you.

2. *Acceptance:* taking pleasure and satisfaction in the whole of who you are, embracing all aspects of yourself.

3. *Self-confidence:* a belief in yourself and in your ability to learn, grow, accomplish goals, solve problems, perform competently, and be secure.

EXERCISE 23: YOUR SELF-CONCEPT

In the following exercise you will define self-concept from the inside out to help you become aware of your intrinsic value. See the *Jumpstart Exercise to help you complete this exercise.*

1. How is your self-confidence tied to the external factors in your life?

2. What do you need to change in order to build your self-confidence from the inside out?

3. What gives you intrinsic self-confidence, beyond things like job, money, home, relationships?

4. Do you sometimes find yourself being overly arrogant or overly self-deprecating?

5. How does being overconfident or underconfident affect your anger management?

6.   How does your self-confidence affect the way you handle anger?

7.   What parts of yourself do you have trouble accepting?

8.   What do you fear most about accepting yourself?

9.   What has to change in order for you to be more self-accepting?

10. If you were more accepting, how would other parts of your life change?

11. How does your self-acceptance affect the way you handle anger?

12. Who are you from the inside out?

13. What qualities best describe who you are?

14. What roles do you take on in daily life?

15. What is your basic character?

16. How does the way you define yourself currently affect your anger management?

17. What needs to change in the way you define who you are in order to better tame your temper?

18. Are you able to appreciate and enjoy yourself?

19. Are you able to appreciate and enjoy others?

20. What needs to change in the way you appreciate yourself?

21. How can a lack of appreciation for self and others affect your anger management?

Jumpstart the Exercise: Kevin's Example

1. How is your self-confidence tied to the external factors in your life?

    I place a lot of importance on being good at my job as a lawyer, on being a good provider, and on being successful compared to other people.

2. What do you need to change in order to build your self-confidence from the inside out?

    I could start by taking work out of my mental equation. I will look at myself, who I am as a person, without making it all about my career. I need to start seeing myself as a valuable human being apart from my career and my income.

3. What gives you intrinsic self-confidence, beyond things like job, money, home, and relationships?

    I get intrinsic value from being a good person—my kindness, my willingness to give love, my openness to learning new things, and my interest in life and growth.

4. Do you sometimes find yourself being overly arrogant or overly self-deprecating?

    I do both things for the same reason: Because I feel inadequate. I sometimes march around telling everyone my accomplishments because I want to feel important and worthy. Other times, I feel despair and I work hard to try to "make up for" my inadequacy. I think negative things about myself when I'm feeling down.

5. How does being overconfident or underconfident affect your anger management?

    When I'm overconfident, I barrel in and make my presence known. Sometimes my bull-headed arrogance creates problems in my relationships and causes fights.

    When I'm underconfident, I get angry because I feel like a victim with no hope. It's frustrating to feel inadequate and ineffective.

6. How does your self-confidence affect the way you handle anger?

    My lack of self-confidence gets me in trouble on either side—either I'm too arrogant or too "poor me." Either one causes me to feel angry and upset.

7. What parts of yourself do you have trouble accepting?

    I have trouble accepting the fact that I am an introvert in a business that requires a great deal of human interaction.

8. What do you fear most about accepting yourself?

    I fear that if I accept myself, then I'm trapping myself into a life of being shy and that I won't mind being a failure.

9. What has to change in order for you to be more self-accepting?

    I need to consider opening my mind to seeing who I am without so much harsh judgment. Maybe I could see being an introvert as a sign of depth rather than as weakness. Maybe I could see my career as one small element in my life instead of as the one major indicator of "Who I Am."

10. If you were more accepting, how would other parts of your life change?

    Well, I might be able to relax and enjoy my life more. I might give myself a chance to be alone without feeling like I should be out networking all of the time. I might feel less pressured at work, and then maybe I would be more productive and satisfied there.

11. How does your self-acceptance affect the way you handle anger?

   If I were more self-accepting, I wouldn't be so frustrated and short-tempered.

12. Who are you from the inside out?

   I am an intelligent guy who means well and who wants to enjoy my life and my loved ones and who wants to learn how to be fully myself.

13. What qualities best describe who you are?

   Frustrated, uncontrolled, fearful, unworthy, aggressive but also reserved, earnest, honest, loyal, loving.

14. What roles do you take on in daily life?

   Lawyer, husband, son, friend.

15. What is your basic character?

   Loyal and kind.

16. How does the way you define yourself currently affect your anger management?

   If I keep seeing myself as unworthy, it makes me forget about those other positive qualities, and I become frustrated and angry.

17. What needs to change in the way you define who you are in order to better tame your temper?

   I need to focus on my good qualities and on my willingness to work on my not-so-good qualities. That's what makes a decent person.

18. Are you able to appreciate and enjoy yourself?

   It depends on the day. Sometimes I feel good and can appreciate and enjoy myself, but not always. Sometimes I just feel terrible, and I can't appreciate or enjoy anything about myself.

19. Are you able to appreciate and enjoy others?

   Yes, I appreciate and enjoy my wife, my parents, and my friends, but sometimes I ruin it when I'm in a bad mood.

20. What needs to change in the way you appreciate yourself?

   I need to learn how not to inflict negativity on myself and on other people. I need to begin to appreciate my good qualities and let those qualities make me better instead of letting my not-so-good qualities bring me down.

21. How can a lack of appreciation for self and others affect your anger management?

   When I'm not being appreciative of myself and others, I get grumpy, angry, or aggressive. That kind of bad mood or behavior doesn't help anything. If I can begin to focus more on what I appreciate about myself and other people, I think I'll be happier and calmer.

◆ WAYS TO BOOST YOUR SELF-CONCEPT

Strategy One: Positive Statements

Take five minutes each day to repeat a few of the following statements to yourself. It will help you focus on your positives rather than the negatives.

"I accept myself fully and completely—my faults, my strengths, my talents, and my challenges."

"I appreciate my own ability to give and receive love."

"Who I am is a considerate, thoughtful, strong, competent person."

"I believe in my ability to problem-solve, see choices, and make decisions."

"I have respect for myself and other people."

"I can control myself and express my feelings calmly and clearly."

"Other people are not my enemies—They are coming from a different perspective, and that's okay."

"I choose collaboration over a win-lose mentality."

At the least, these affirmations will force you to actually **think** about concepts like being considerate, thoughtful, and competent. And they just might make you believe those things could be true about you. The more you practice saying them, the truer they seem and the more you will see evidence of your good qualities in your daily life. As you say, "I accept myself fully and completely," you may feel yourself relax and unwind. Such a deceptively easy practice can make a huge difference in your self-concept.

Strategy Two: Take Healthy Risks

Overcome your fear of rejection by softening your approach to other people. (Smile, say hello, be friendly and open.)

Do something nice for yourself, such as going to a spa, exercising, napping, reading a book, going to an art museum, taking a bubble bath, or attending a sporting event.

Focus on your own needs by not spreading yourself too thin, not overcommitting, and not overextending yourself. Take time for solitude to recharge your battery.

Do something outside your comfort zone—expand your horizons by taking a class, doing a new activity, exploring new culture and new ideas.

Have the confidence to reenter an old argument from a new angle—Be willing to overcome your fear of past negative outcomes by showing that you care enough to negotiate with others.

EXERCISE 24: TAKE AN INVENTORY

See the *Jumpstart Exercise to help you complete this exercise.*

1. Take a Personal Inventory

YOUR STRENGTHS	YOUR WEAKNESSES

2. Now that you have taken a personal inventory, make a plan to improve each weakness by coming up with specific strategies.

WEAKNESS:

a) Strength that will help me overcome my weakness:

b) Plan for overcoming weakness:

c) Timetable for overcoming weakness:

d) Successful completion of improvement plan:

Jumpstart the Exercise: Kevin's Example

STRENGTHS	WEAKNESSES
Loyal	*Frustrated*
Earnest	*Uncontrolled*
Honest	*Fearful*
Loving	*Unworthy/Inadequate*
Reserved/Deep	*Aggressive*

WEAKNESS: *Aggressive*

a) Strength that will help me overcome my weakness: *Being a loving person*

b) Plan for overcoming weakness:

I'm going to remind myself to behave in more loving ways, to love myself more, and to love other people more. The more loving I feel, the less likely I am to behave aggressively. There are other things I can do, too, like exercising, deep breathing, and releasing muscle tension, which will help me to manage my tendency to be aggressive.

c) Timetable for overcoming weakness:

This will be an ongoing process, but I expect to show improvement within the next two weeks.

d) Successful completion of improvement plan:

I will seek feedback from my wife and from my parents to see if my plan is making progress. I will keep an eye on my attitude so that I will stay loving and unaggressive as a lifelong practice.

WEAKNESS: *Feeling unworthy or inadequate*

    a)   Strength that will help me overcome my weakness:

        All of them—my honesty, my loyalty, my earnestness, my loving attitude, and my depth of introspection.

    b)   Plan for overcoming weakness:

        I will use daily affirmations and remember all of my better qualities to combat my tendency to feel unworthy. I will focus on the positive parts of who I am. I will challenge my negative automatic thoughts.

    c)   Timetable for overcoming weakness:

        This will be an ongoing process, but I expect to show improvement within the next two weeks.

    d)   Successful completion of improvement plan:

        I will know that I am succeeding when my thoughts are not dominated by the topic of "Not Being Good Enough." I will feel more confident and adequate. I will take on new challenges and others close to me will be able to see the improvement.

PASSIVE, AGGRESSIVE, AND ASSERTIVE COMMUNICATION

The three most common styles of expressing anger are passive, aggressive, or assertive.

1. **Passive:** Expressing feelings indirectly and in a way that comes across as weak and self-denying. Sulking or acting self-pitying are examples of passive communication. So is acting out by getting drunk or overeating. It's the "poor me" approach.

2. **Aggressive:** Conveying feelings in a way that disregards the rights of others. Using verbal threats, intimidation, and physical force are forms of aggressive communication.

3. **Assertive:** Communicating feelings in a way that is direct, self-respecting, honest, sensitive, and values the rights of others.

Remember our friend Bob, who was angry when he saw his girlfriend dancing with another guy? If Bob communicated assertively, he would wait respectfully during most of the song, then approach his girlfriend on the dance floor to politely request to cut in. In the car on the way home later, he would talk with her about his anxious and jealous feelings. He would express to her in a calm, conversational tone that he felt somewhat hurt and angry, even though he knew that was not her intention.

Clearly, assertive communication is the healthiest, most effective approach. If you can present your feelings and thoughts in a way that is self-respecting, sensitive, direct, and nonthreatening, you will not only resolve your disputes but build trust and closeness with the other person—money in the bank against future disputes.

EXERCISE 25: YOUR COMMUNICATION STYLE

Think about the last two times you were extremely angry, and use the format below to determine your usual communication approach. See the *Jumpstart Exercise to help complete your own.*

SITUATION 1

Briefly describe a situation.

Based on the above definitions, what approach did you apply in this situation?

Passive   Aggressive   Assertive

If this was not an assertive response, what prevented you from being assertive?

- Was I feeling fear?
- Was I feeling a need for power and control?
- Was I feeling rejected?
- Was I feeling hurt?
- Was I feeling a sense of inadequacy?
- Was I feeling exposed?

- Did I fear change?
- Was I feeling helpless?
- Was I feeling confused?
- Was I feeling guilty?
- Was I feeling manipulated?
- Were there other obstacles that prevented you from being assertive?

ADDITIONAL THOUGHTS:

Check below how you could have responded in an assertive manner.

COULD YOU HAVE…

- Spoken up for myself in a respectful way?

- Been more forthright about my feelings?

- Refused to wallow in self-pity?

- Stood up for myself without being disrespectful?

- Owned up to my own uncomfortable feelings?

- Made my wishes known?

- Been more willing to displease someone?

- Protected my own boundaries?

- Approached the situation directly and respectfully?

- Additional thoughts:

- Asked to hear the other person's perspective?

- Waited for an appropriate moment to discuss the conflict?

- Been more willing to listen to other opinions?

- Slowed myself down so that I could think more clearly?

- Been more open to compromise?

- Conveyed a sense that I respected the rights of others?

- Expressed a willingness to be sensitive to others while maintaining my own boundaries?

SITUATION 2

Briefly describe a situation.

Based on the above definitions, what approach did you apply in this situation?

Passive   Aggressive   Assertive

If this was not an assertive response, what prevented you from being assertive?

- Was I feeling fear?

- Was I feeling a need for power and control?

- Was I feeling rejected?

- Was I feeling hurt?

- Was I feeling a sense of inadequacy?

- Was I feeling exposed?

- Did I fear change?

- Was I feeling helpless?

- Was I feeling confused?

- Was I feeling guilty?

- Was I feeling manipulated?

- Were there other obstacles that prevented you from being assertive?

ADDITIONAL THOUGHTS:

Check below how you could have responded in an assertive manner.

COULD YOU HAVE...

- Spoken up for myself in a respectful way?
- Been more forthright about my feelings?
- Refused to wallow in self-pity?
- Stood up for myself without being disrespectful?
- Owned up to my own uncomfortable feelings?
- Made my wishes known?
- Been more willing to displease someone?
- Protected my own boundaries?
- Approached the situation directly and respectfully?
- Additional thoughts:

- Asked to hear the other person's perspective?
- Waited for an appropriate moment to discuss the conflict?
- Been more willing to listen to other opinions?
- Slowed myself down so that I could think more clearly?
- Been more open to compromise?
- Conveyed a sense that I respected the rights of others?
- Expressed a willingness to be sensitive to others while maintaining my own boundaries?

Jumpstart the Exercise: Bob's Example

Situation 1

> *I saw my girlfriend dancing with another guy. I marched onto the dance floor, grabbed her, and threatened the guy.*

Based on the above definitions, what approach are you applying in this situation?

Passive   **Aggressive**   Assertive

If this was not an assertive response, what prevented you from being assertive?

- Was I feeling fear? *Yes, fear of losing my girlfriend*
- Was I feeling a need for power and control? *Yes, because I felt out of control*
- Was I feeling rejected? *Yes, I wanted to dance with her myself*
- Was I feeling hurt? *Yes*
- Was I feeling a sense of inadequacy? *Absolutely*
- Was I feeling exposed? *Not really*

- Did I fear change? *Maybe*
- Was I feeling helpless? *Yes, at first*
- Was I feeling confused? *Yes*
- Was I feeling guilty? *No*
- Was I feeling manipulated? *I'm not sure, maybe*
- Were there other obstacles that prevented you from being assertive? *I felt like I needed to restore my power, my dignity, and my pride*

- Additional Thoughts: *I could have been less impulsive. I could have waited, politely cut in, danced with my girlfriend, and maybe talked calmly about my feelings later when we were alone. I could have given her a chance to explain.*

Situation 2

> *The mailman keeps bringing the wrong mail to my house and then leaving **my** mail at my neighbor's house. I've even had some overdue bills because of how often he makes this mistake. Last Saturday, I waited until I saw him come up to my mailbox. I ran outside and told him off, threatened to get him fired, and I even told him that if he messed up again, I would kick his butt. He looked like he thought I was crazy. I'm not crazy, but I am very frustrated.*

Based on the above definitions, what approach are you applying in this situation?

Passive   **Aggressive**   Assertive

If this was not an assertive response, what prevented you from being assertive?

- Was I feeling fear? *Maybe—fearful of being behind on my bills*
- Was I feeling rejected? *No*
- Was I feeling hurt? *No*
- Was I feeling a sense of inadequacy? *Sort of—I was embarrassed about late bill payments*

- Was I feeling exposed? *No, I don't think so*
- Did I fear change? *No*
- Was I feeling helpless? *Yes, because I can't control the mail*
- Was I feeling confused? *Some—I don't understand why he can't get it right*
- Was I feeling guilty? *No*

- Was I feeling manipulated? *No*

- Were there other obstacles that prevented you from being assertive? *I was feeling very frustrated and impatient*

- Additional Thoughts:

  I could have been more polite. I didn't have to threaten the mailman. I could have explained my problem to him and hoped that things would improve. If they didn't improve, I could have contacted his supervisor at the post office.

LETTING GO

When you're hurt or angry, you call on your defense mechanisms to keep anxiety, anger, and fear at bay. But in reality, most defense mechanisms lock us into negative emotions by preventing us from letting go of unpleasant memories. Defense mechanisms include rumination, fight rehearsal, grudges, isolating, and looking for patterns.

1. **Rumination** is pushing the "rewind button" on old misunderstandings and perceived hurts, or repeating a fight in your mind over and over to the point of obsession.

    Example: Joe has a fight with his wife. He keeps rehashing the argument in his head for hours afterward. Joe ruminates because he doesn't want to forget how badly he was hurt or to be caught off guard next time. Joe is afraid to let go.

2. **Fight Rehearsal** is fantasizing about a future fight, preparing your argument in advance, visualizing what you will do or say, and planning your strategy to win.

    Example: Kim and her sister have an argument, but Kim never really says her piece. Later at home, Kim furiously visualizes their next fight, plans what she will say, and imagines how she will get her point across. Kim thinks her angry insistence on "imaginary fight rehearsal" will ensure that she will be heard in the future. But all it does is keep her from letting go.

3. **Grudges** are when you refuse to forgive, forget, or show compassion or empathy for someone else's mistakes, perspective, or differences.

    Example: Sarah's mother-in-law, Judy, did not attend her son's wedding to Sarah because she had an emergency surgery that day. Since then, Judy has been helpful, polite, and welcoming to Sarah. However, Sarah refuses to forget the perceived slight—she frequently refers to the fact that Judy missed the wedding, reminds her husband about his mom's absence, and will not forgive Judy for her offense. Though she may imagine that this behavior protects her from future disappointment, Sarah's holding on to a grudge keeps her mother-in-law at arm's length.

4. **Isolating** means walking away from a discussion, giving the silent treatment, or guarding yourself against further hurt by withholding emotionally and physically.

    Example: Richard, the executor of his dad's will, reluctantly carried out his duties. His twin brother, Steve, felt excluded from the process. Since then, Steve refuses to visit Richard at holidays, won't speak to him at family reunions, and doesn't return Richard's phone calls. Steve is isolating and withholding in an attempt to avoid conflict or future pain at the cost of a relationship with his brother.

5. **Looking for Patterns** is looking for similar memories, behaviors, or interactions to hold against someone. You are trying to support your theory that this is not a one-time problem, but a major recurring issue in the relationship.

    Example: John forgot Valentine's Day once, in 1999. Since then, his wife Margaret has labeled John as a forgetful, thoughtless husband. Anytime a holiday is nearing, Margaret starts paying close attention to whether John remembers it, mentions it, or seems excited about it. In addition, Margaret watches John with an eagle eye for other areas where John might be forgetful, such as with grocery lists, taking out the trash, or relaying phone messages. Margaret is "pattern-searching" because she is fearful of being hurt again and wants to be prepared next time. But it adds a bitter and accusatory tone to the marriage.

- **_Rumination:_** Give yourself a time limit on the ruminating so that you don't get stuck replaying the recent conflict. You might tell yourself, "I will allow myself to replay the fight for the next five minutes and then I will go take a run." Now take a few minutes to come up with your own replacement behaviors for the problem of rumination.

- **_Fight rehearsal:_** Create a new, more positive narrative as you engage in imaginary fight rehearsal. If you must visualize future arguments, imagine yourself communicating respectfully, listening attentively, and resolving the conflict successfully. Now generate some more ways to create a positive, constructive narrative.

- **_Grudges:_** Challenge yourself to show greater emotional generosity. When you catch yourself holding a grudge, try instead to ask yourself, "What is the payoff from holding on to this grudge?" Also ask yourself, "How might this grudge impact my own emotional health?" Imagine what it would feel like to release yourself from the burden of holding this grudge. Think of some more options for releasing grudges.

- **_Isolating/withholding:_** Take a limited time-out. After taking a reasonable break to think about the situation, challenge yourself to make a concerted effort to reengage in a constructive discussion about the conflict. Be available to resolve the problem, rather than checking out to avoid future pain. Next, come up with some additional ways to stop yourself from isolating.

- **_Pattern-searching:_** Stay away from overgeneralizing ("you always," "you never"), and keep in mind that people are human and can make mistakes. Remember that it is possible for people to learn, develop, and change. Discipline yourself to stay in the present, and tackle each topic individually. Generate your own list of alternatives to pattern-searching.

◈ SIX STEPS FOR LETTING GO

Think of a situation that has made you lose your temper in the past. Then use these six steps to let go of it once and for all. What a relief!

1. Identify which defense mechanisms are preventing you from letting go.

2. Be accountable. Admit how you have contributed to the conflict and how your unhealthy safety behaviors might be keeping you locked into the conflict.

3. Show empathy. Consider the other person's position—his or her needs, fears, and perspective.

4. Accept your differences and value those differences. Be willing to open your mind to thoughts, behaviors, and feelings that don't match your own. Remember we are all different, unique individuals.

5. Generate healthy behaviors to replace the unhealthy defense mechanisms.

6. Forgive. Forgiveness has two sides—giving and receiving. On the giving side, you are offering forgiveness to someone else. On the receiving side, you are asking another person for forgiveness for yourself. When offering forgiveness, keep the concepts of kindness and mercy in your thoughts. Remember that no one is perfect and work toward understanding the other person more deeply.

When asking for forgiveness, be clear about the offense itself, show willingness to imagine how the other person might be feeling, take responsibility for the wrongs you have done, and pledge to improve your own behavior. Explain how you plan to avoid similar problems in the future and respectfully ask for forgiveness.

TIME MANAGEMENT

People with fuzzy boundaries almost always struggle with time. They don't know how to protect their own time from the demands of others. They spend their finite time with infinite abandon, and they wind up abandoning themselves. The more ineffective with protecting our time we are, the more likely to feel angry, pressed, and overwhelmed trying to meet daily demands. This can lead to procrastination, which creates even more stress, tension, powerlessness, and anxiety. Consistent procrastination leads to anger by increasing your sense of urgency, impatience, and frustration. If you can set limits around your time, it will help you avoid becoming overwhelmed, decrease your frustration, increase your energy, and provide stability. Your boundaries will naturally strengthen. See the ***Jumpstart Exercise to help you complete this exercise.***

EXERCISE 26: YOUR TIME-MANAGEMENT SKILLS

1. Take an inventory of how you handle time

    a) Where and how do you spend the majority of your time?

    b) Are you frustrated by the current distribution of how you spend your time?

    c) Do you let other people manage your time for you?

    d) Do you consistently take time for yourself?

    e) Do you find yourself resenting the time you spend on specific areas of your life? If so, which ones?

f) What other thoughts come up as you think about the issue of time in your daily life?

2. Address Procrastination

   a) Do you wait until the last minute to complete tasks?

   b) Do you find yourself rushing when trying to complete daily tasks?

   c) Do you postpone important conversations?

   d) Do you delay your goals?

   e) Do you put off personal activities?

f) Do you drag your feet in regard to tackling responsibilities?

g) Do you find yourself rearranging your schedule at the last minute to accommodate urgent situations?

Jumpstart the Exercise: Carol's Example

1. Take an inventory of how you handle time.

   a) Where and how do you spend the majority of your time?

   At work.

   b) Are you frustrated by the current distribution of how you spend your time?

   Yes, I feel overwhelmed by work.

   c) Do you let other people manage your time for you?

   Sometimes, yes. If my supervisor offers me overtime, I always say yes. Then, I end up working weekends.

   d) Do you consistently take time for yourself?

   It depends on how you look at it. I do tend to isolate myself when I feel overwhelmed, so I do spend time alone but it's not always positive self-care. I might feel better if I planned to do some things I enjoy when I am alone.

   e) Do you find yourself resenting the time you spend on specific areas of your life? If so, which ones?

   I resent my job, and I resent that I don't get to spend as much time with my friends and family. Once, I missed a family funeral just because I was working an extra shift.

   f) What other thoughts come up as you think about the issue of time in your daily life?

   I let work dominate my clock. I need to change that.

2. Address Procrastination

   a) Do you wait until the last minute to complete tasks?

   No, not at work. I put my relationships on hold in order to get my work done.

   b) Do you find yourself rushing when trying to complete daily tasks?

   Yes, I rush because I've overfilled my plate. I've got too much to do and not enough time to do it.

   c) Do you postpone important conversations?

   Yes, sometimes I avoid difficult talks with my friends or family because I'm too tired from work to focus. I just don't want to start a big discussion when I am tired. Once, I fell asleep on the phone in the middle of my friend trying to talk to me about her feelings.

   d) Do you delay your goals?

   I delay getting in shape because I don't have time to exercise.

   e) Do you put off personal activities?

   Yes. I want to visit my mom, travel to the Grand Canyon, learn to knit, and so on . . . but my work gets in the way.

   f) Do you drag your feet in regard to tackling responsibilities?

   Not at work. I drag my feet on personal matters. It has been three years since my last dental checkup, for example.

   g) Do you find yourself rearranging your schedule at the last minute to accommodate urgent situations?

   Almost never. I don't rearrange things, even when I should.

HOW TO SET BETTER TIME LIMITS

Use Four-Part "I" Statements to Set Limits
1. Start the sentence with an "I" for ownership.

2. Tell how you feel about the behavior.

3. Define the behavior.

4. Describe how the behavior affects you.

> *For example,* "*I* (**Start sentence with I for ownership**) *feel stressed* (**how you feel about the behavior**) *when things get put on my calendar without me being consulted* (**define the behavior**), *because I end up double booking myself* (**describe how the behavior affects you**)."
>
> More examples of four-part "I-statements":
>
> *I know you like to watch television at night. Unfortunately, I tend to have trouble sleeping with the television on. How can we solve this conflict in a fair way?*
>
> *I know you love your mother, and I'm fond of her, too. I want to be able to enjoy her visits, so I was wondering if we could limit her visits to a few days.*

Setting Expectations on Time
A great way to set limits is to let others know up front in a courteous way how you would like to spend your time.

- Set expectations with others about how you spend your work and downtime. For example, let others know not to call you at work. Or tell your spouse that sometimes you would like a "girls/guys night out."

- Start a new relationship by letting your partner know how much time you'd like to spend together versus apart. For example, say, "Usually, when I'm dating someone, I like to spend at least one day of the weekend together. How about you?"

- Reestablish expectations in an established relationship with a conversation about the future. For instance, say to your boss, "I know you've always expected me to work on Saturdays, and I've enjoyed doing it. Now I want to take a business class to help develop my leadership skills. The class is held on Saturday mornings. I would like to work out a new schedule with you for the next 10 weeks to accommodate my goal. I would be willing to work late on Thursdays to make up for the time lost on Saturdays."

Expressing Needs, Thoughts, and Desires
Very often others are quite happy to accommodate your limits as long as they know and understand what they are.

- Communicate a limit with someone by expressing your needs. For example, a mom might tell her children, *I want to reconnect with you, but I also need 30 minutes of downtime when I get home from work before you start telling me about your day. If you can wait 30 minutes, I'm all yours.*

- Give voice to your thoughts. A man might say to his mother, *I've been thinking we talk about the weather a lot. Next time I come over for dinner, I would love it if you would tell me about what it was like for you when you were raising me as a single mom with no help or if I could tell you more about my job and my hobbies.*

- Convey a limit by opening up about your desires. A young woman might tell her boyfriend, *I really need more time to myself in the mornings. I wonder if it would be okay with you if I spend a few mornings doing yoga and meditation before we start our errands and chores.*

LETTING GO OF UNHEALTHY RELATIONSHIPS

Letting go of unhealthy relationships is one of the most difficult limits to set. Verbally acknowledge to another person that you will need to let go of your friendship because it is emotionally draining or counter-productive. For example, you might say, "It is clear that our lives have taken different paths. I think we should spend more time apart."

Try to state your intention to let go of certain activities, like gossip, excessive drinking, or gambling. You could say to your neighbor, "I enjoy our friendship, and I want it to continue. Lately, it seems like our conversations have become more like gossip, and I think we're short-changing ourselves. I would love it if we could discuss our lives, our thoughts, and our plans instead. Want to get together on Thursday and talk?"

Verbally declare that you would like to discontinue outdated or unhelpful habits, like wasting time on the Internet, excessive television-watching, or disproportionate people-pleasing. A spouse could say, "I tend to fall into the habit of watching television with you for hours every night. I think I might be happier if we watched less TV and played more board games. I would like it very much if you wanted to try that with me this week."

RIGHTS AND RESPONSIBILITIES

Our understanding of our rights and responsibilities plays a major part in how we set boundaries. Knowing your rights and being responsible will help improve the way you deal with conflict, manage anger, and handle your relationships.

RIGHTS

- I have the right to say no.

- I have the right to respect.

- I have the right to state my needs.

- I have the right to state my desires.

- I have the right to experience my own feelings.

- I have the right to my own ideas and thoughts.

- I have the right to define my own personal space.

- I have the right to physical safety.

- I have the right to say "yes" or "no" to sexual contact.

- I have the right to choose my personal relationships.

- I have the right to define how I spend my personal time.

- I have a right to make choices regarding my body and my health.

- I have a right to my own orientation, religion, political views, and beliefs.

RESPONSIBILITIES

- I have the responsibility not to physically harm another person.

- I have the responsibility to respect others.

- I have the responsibility to be open to differences.

- I have the responsibility to listen to others.

- I have the responsibility to respect another person's decision regarding sexual contact.

- I have the responsibility to respect others' personal space.

- I have the responsibility to respect others when they say "No."

- I have the responsibility to communicate as clearly as possible.

- I have the responsibility to be nonthreatening to others.

- I have the responsibility to stay away from criticizing, blaming, or minimizing.

- I have the responsibility to be accountable for my own behavior.

- I have the responsibility to be compassionate toward myself and others.

- I have the responsibility to be forgiving toward myself and others.

- I have the responsibility to be gracious toward myself and others.

- I have the responsibility to speak to others respectfully without yelling or raising my voice.

- I have the responsibility not to throw things, slam doors, punch walls, spit, or display violent behavior.

- I have the responsibility to express myself without being secretive, hiding, or concealing my feelings.

- I have the responsibility to work on letting go of past offenses.

- I have the responsibility not to dwell on the negative or to ruminate.

EXERCISE 27: YOUR RIGHTS AND RESPONSIBILITIES

VIOLATING ANOTHER PERSON'S RIGHTS

1. Describe a time when you violated the rights of someone else. What happened? How did you feel? How did the other person respond?

2. Was there a more constructive way to handle the situation? If yes, think about how you will address similar issues in the future. You can utilize the list of rights above to guide you.

YOUR OWN RIGHTS

1. Write about a time when your rights were violated. What happened? How did you feel? How did you respond? What was the outcome?

2. How will you handle future situations when your rights are being violated?

MISMANAGING YOUR RESPONSIBILITIES

1. Describe a situation in which you were unsuccessful in managing your responsibilities toward yourself or others. What happened? How did you feel? What got in the way of you being more responsible?

2. How will you be more responsible toward yourself in the future?

3. How will you be more responsible toward others in the future?

Jumpstart the Exercise: Dan's Example

VIOLATING ANOTHER PERSON'S RIGHTS

1. Describe a time when you violated the rights of someone else. What happened? How did you feel? How did the other person respond?

   I was at a bar, saving a seat for my friend. A woman came over and asked to borrow the barstool, and I exploded—told her to go to hell, that the seat was for my friend. I violated the rights of the lady by yelling at her for no good reason. I behaved disrespectfully. I was very angry at the time, but felt embarrassed later. The woman walked away in tears.

2. Was there a more constructive way to handle the situation? If yes, think about how you will address similar issues in the future. You can utilize the list of rights above to guide you.

   I could have respected the lady's right to use the barstool. I could have respected her right not to be spoken to in a threatening manner, and I could have been more responsible for the way I commu¬nicated.

YOUR OWN RIGHTS

1. Write about a time when your rights were violated. What happened? How did you feel? How did you respond? What was the outcome?

   I got passed over for a promotion. I felt humiliated and inadequate. I responded by burying myself in more work, to prove I was the better man for the job. I ended up feeling resentful, but no one knew it. I wasn't assertive with my boss.

2. How will you handle future situations when your rights are being violated?

   I will find an appropriate and respectful way to communicate. I'll ask my boss to help me understand why they hired someone else. I'll work hard, but I won't overdo it.

MISMANAGING YOUR RESPONSIBILITIES

1. Describe a situation in which you were unsuccessful in managing your responsibilities toward yourself or others. What happened? How did you feel? What got in the way of you being more responsible?

   I wasn't very responsible in the way I yelled at my girlfriend when I was angry. We were talking about money, and I blew up. I felt I was being criticized, but I didn't say so. I just verbally attacked her, loudly. My own pride and fear got in the way of being more responsible.

2. How will you be more responsible toward yourself in the future?

   If I were to be more responsible toward myself, I would remember to respect my own needs, my own ability to communicate in a fair way, and not to shortchange myself when it comes to being an adult. I can be as mature as anyone else, and I need to remember that and act that way—for my own self-respect.

3. How will you be more responsible toward others in the future?

   I'm going to work on my vocal volume. It isn't effective or respectful when I scream and yell. I'm going to improve the way I handle conversations.

CHAPTER FIVE

Taming Your Temper: The Life Plan

Taming your temper is a lifelong program: You don't "graduate," although it does get easier and more automatic with practice. I've noticed that unless clients *continue* to take excellent care of their basic needs, assess their overall satisfaction, and have a robust support circle, they will backslide as quickly as you can say, "Oh no here we go again." It's like building a house: You can paint it a pretty color, put up nice curtains, and buy comfortable furniture, and it may look good from the outside. But unless you have a strong foundation and a watertight roof, all your work will come crumbling down or be ruined by the next big storm. Regular maintenance work is equally essential in keeping up a home—and a healthy home life.

In this chapter, you will have a chance to keep looking at balancing your needs, to solidify all the gains you've already made, and to keep up the great work.

HOW TO STAY IN BALANCE: YOUR ESSENTIAL NEEDS

Most people would agree that good nutrition, exercise, and sleep are basic human needs. I would add prayer, meditation, and gratitude to that list. When your basic life needs are out of balance, handling your anger in a healthy way can be much harder. When you are meeting your basic needs, you feel stable, centered, and calm. You'll be better able to handle anger and less likely to slip back into unhealthy habits.

You've no doubt seen the government nutrition pyramid, illustrating the role each kind of food plays in building good physical health. The basic needs pyramid below shows the building blocks you need to maintain good emotional, mental, physical, and spiritual health.

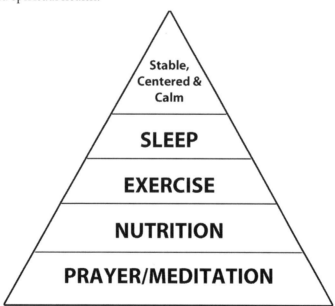

Strengthening your own basic needs pyramid—those elements of your life that keep you on an even keel—will give you the stability to keep your anger under control. Basic needs do much more than help ward off anger. They are essential to your physical health. They maximize your opportunities for good social encounters, and they increase feelings of happiness. Individual pyramids can vary from person to person. For you, sleep might be your most important component of anger prevention; nutrition might be your wife's biggest priority.

The basic needs exercises are like an anger prevention program. Each exercise allows you to customize the building blocks and then helps you chart your progress.

Take some time to organize your basic needs pyramid. Start with the pyramid's foundation and consider which component is a priority. Is getting enough sleep most important in managing your emotions? Then place sleep at the bottom of the pyramid. After you've completed your pyramid, you are ready to tackle the exercises that follow to improve each area.

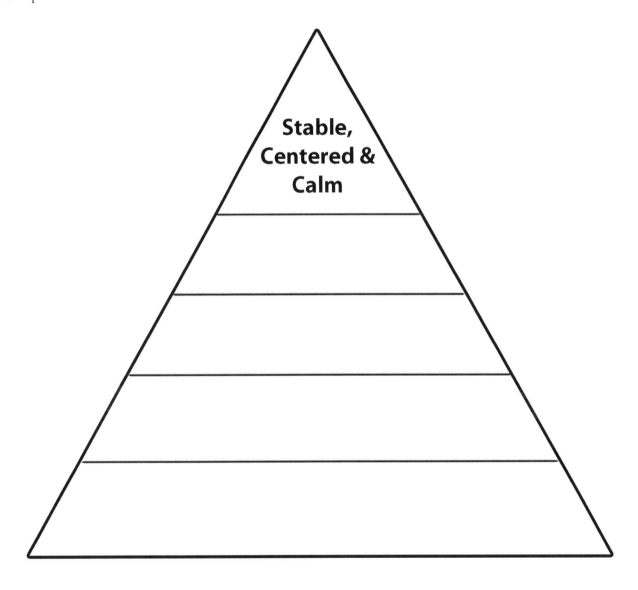

EXERCISE 28: PHYSICAL ACTIVITY FOR ANGER PREVENTION

Whenever possible, add exercise to your daily routine. Document your physical activity each day, writing down either "No exercise today," or "Walked 30 minutes," "Went for a run," "Played basketball," and so on. Each day, regardless of whether you exercised, make sure to record your anger level, circling a number between 0 and 3. Use the following chart.

Anger Level Key   3=High   2=Moderate   1=Mild   0=Calm

Day	Exercise	Anger Level
Sun		3 2 1 0
Mon		3 2 1 0
Tue		3 2 1 0
Wed		3 2 1 0
Thur		3 2 1 0
Fri		3 2 1 0
Sat		3 2 1 0

Weekly Anger Levels

Calculate your weekly anger level by adding up each day's total, regardless of whether you have stuck with the exercise plan. Watch to see how exercise affects your ability to manage anger.

- **0-10 Calm and Balanced**—At this level, you're managing your anger effectively through daily exercise. Continue doing what you're doing as a way to stay stable, centered and calm.

- **11-14 Moderate Anger Levels**—At this level, your physical activity is probably inadequate. You might decide to exercise more, change the type of exercise you're doing, or seek out a professional trainer.

- **15-21 High Anger Levels**—At this level, it's likely that many parts of your life are out of balance. It's therefore even more crucial to incorporate regular exercise into your routine. If your levels are consistently high, you might want to seek professional help from a therapist or psychiatrist.

NUTRITION FOR ANGER PREVENTION

Nutrition can have a major impact on how you cope with anger. You are likely to get into more arguments if you have eaten junk foods or skipped a meal.

EXERCISE 29: YOUR NUTRITION INVENTORY

1. Do you eat from the four basic food groups (dairy, meat/protein, grain, fruits and vegetables)?

2. Do you drink water and stay hydrated?

3. Do you consume mostly healthy fats, such as polyunsaturated and monounsaturated fats (fish, avocado, walnuts, olive oil, soybean oil, and flaxseed)?

4. Do you try to avoid trans-fats in your diet, such as cookies, crackers, pies, donuts, and fried items?

5. Do you eat more complex carbohydrates (vegetables, whole grain cereal, and whole wheat pasta) than simple carbohydrates (fruit juice, milk, white bread, white rice, sugar)?

6. Do you get enough protein (poultry, fish, tofu, beans, and nuts) in your diet?

7. Are you careful not to skip meals?

8. Do you limit your caffeine intake?

9. Do you limit your sugar intake?

10. Do you make sure to eat moderately—enough to keep you active but not so much that you become sluggish?

EVALUATING YOUR NUTRITION

If you answered "Yes" to all of these questions, then your nutrition is in excellent condition.

If you answered "No" to any of these questions, then there's room for improvement. As you begin to eat healthier foods, you'll feel healthier and more in control. Your anger fuse will be much longer, and you'll be more open to taking the time you need to resolve a conflict.

Each week, take one of your "No" answers and work to change it to a "Yes." Add one new positive habit each week. At the end of each week, track your anger levels. See how the improvements in your nutrition correspond with your ability to manage your anger.

Use the accompanying blank log to track your anger levels over time as you improve your nutrition:

Your Weekly Nutritional Changes Log: Impact on Anger Levels

Anger Level	10 Weeks									
	1	2	3	4	5	6	7	8	9	10
Intense Anger										
Moderate Anger										
Mild Anger										
Calm										

Jumpstart the Exercise: Bill's Example

Anger Level	10 Weeks									
	1	2	3	4	5	6	7	8	9	10
Intense Anger			▓							
Moderate Anger	▓	▓		▓	▓					
Mild Anger						▓			▓	
Calm							▓	▓		▓

SLEEP FOR ANGER PREVENTION

Sleep, without a doubt, affects how we cope with anger. If you're tired, you're more likely to be cranky or short-tempered—almost any little thing could set you off. Improving your sleep, therefore, can also help improve how you manage anger. If you maintain good sleep habits, you are more likely to feel rested and ready to handle problems calmly as they arise.

EXERCISE 30: YOUR SLEEP INVENTORY

1. Do you maintain a regular bedtime and wake-up time?

2. Do you keep your bedroom dark, cool, and free of distractions?

3. Do you have comfortable bedding and pillows?

4. Do you avoid caffeine in the afternoon?

5. Do you discontinue eating two to three hours before bedtime?

6. Do you avoid watching television an hour before bedtime?

7. Do you avoid working on your computer an hour before bedtime?

8. Do you have a regular relaxing bedtime routine?

9. Do you exercise earlier in the day and relax more near bedtime?

10. If you wake up in the middle of the night, can you gently allow yourself to go back to sleep?

If you answered "Yes" to all of these questions, then you are maintaining excellent sleep habits.

If you answered "No" to any of the questions, then you need to establish better sleep habits. Start your new program *tonight*. You'll soon notice an improvement not only in your sleep but in how you cope with things during the day. Each day, chart your "sleep quality" on a scale of 1 to 10 (1 = no sleep, 10 = excellent sleep) and then chart your anger level for that day. After you have begun your new sleep program, pay attention to how your sleep habits affect your anger levels.

Track how sleep affects your anger levels and your ability to cope with anger by filling out the chart.

Your Daily Sleep Log: Impact on Daily Anger Levels

	Sun	Mon	Tues	Wed	Thurs	Fri	Sat
Sleep Quality							
Intense Anger							
Moderate Anger							
Mild Anger							
Calm							

Jumpstart the Exercise: Bob's Example

	Sun	Mon	Tues	Wed	Thurs	Fri	Sat
Sleep Quality	3	5	6	5	7	8	9
Intense Anger	▓						
Moderate Anger		▓		▓			
Mild Anger			▓		▓		
Calm						▓	▓

SPIRITUALITY FOR ANGER PREVENTION

Even if you do not consider yourself a spiritual person, consider giving prayer, meditation, and gratitude a try. They can have a powerful effect on your overall sense of well-being and ability to tame your temper. Whether spiritual practice is at the top or bottom of your basic needs pyramid, I ask you to at least try the four exercises I've described. Once you've done that, stick with what you like and feel free to leave the rest. I can almost guarantee they will lead to serenity. And if you are serene, it's a lot harder to blow your top!

Daily Spirituality

Choose a spiritual practice and commit to it on a daily basis. Whether it's prayer, meditation, or contemplative reflection, it should fit your sensibility. You might decide on a traditional prayer, a religious observance, or a less conventional option. Perhaps you are most comfortable sitting quietly in nature for a few minutes each day.

As you begin a prayer routine, you might notice that you are improving your ability to manage daily irritations and angry situations, and that you are less likely to fall back into escalating problems. One way to track your progress is by plotting your anger levels on a graph.

EXERCISE 31: YOUR DAILY SPIRITUAL PRACTICE CHART

On Sunday, color in the block that corresponds with your anger level. Write in this chart each week and then compare your anger levels at the end of each month.

As you continue your practice of Daily Prayer, pay attention to how your anger rises and falls each day. Notice your overall trend—are you becoming calmer in general? Would you like to add a second daily prayer at the end or beginning of each day to help create an even greater sense of calm?

Spirituality Practice Chart

	Sun	Mon	Tues	Wed	Thurs	Fri	Sat
Daily Prayer							
Intense Anger							
Moderate Anger							
Mild Anger							
Calm							

Jumpstart the Exercise: Steve's Example

	Sun	Mon	Tues	Wed	Thurs	Fri	Sat
Daily Prayer	X		X	X	X		X
Intense Anger	▓	▓					
Moderate Anger				▓			
Mild Anger			▓		▓	▓	
Calm							▓

METTA MEDITATION

Some people prefer meditation, rather than traditional prayer. One useful meditation is called "Metta Meditation," which incorporates a Buddhist loving-kindness practice combined with relaxation and visualization techniques. Here's how to do a simple Metta Meditation:

- Sit comfortably in a peaceful place. Breathe deeply and relax.

- Start by creating a sense of acceptance for yourself. Say *May I be happy, may I be healthy, may I be free from harm, may I be at peace.*

- Next, visualize a dear friend or loved one, and repeat the phrasing *May (insert name here) be happy, may ___ be healthy, may ___ be free from harm, may ___ be at peace.*

- Next, visualize a more distant person (for instance, the postman) and begin *May the postman be happy, may the postman be healthy, may the postman be free from harm, may the postman be at peace.*

- Then, visualize an enemy or someone with whom you are in conflict: *May (insert name here) be happy, may ___ be healthy, may ___be free from harm, may ___ be at peace.*

- Finally, visualize the world itself, and repeat *May the world be happy, may the world be healthy, may the world be free from harm, may the world be at peace.*

EXERCISE 32: YOUR METTA MEDITATION

This exercise creates a sense of loving-kindness and acceptance of yourself, of your loved ones, of strangers, of your enemies, and of the world. Practice this meditation on a daily basis and fill in the Anger Tracking chart.

	Sun	Mon	Tues	Wed	Thurs	Fri	Sat
Meditation							
Intense Anger							
Moderate Anger							
Mild Anger							
Calm							

GRATITUDE JOURNAL

For those who are not comfortable with prayer or meditation or other spiritual practices, a simple statement of gratitude can be life changing. End or begin each day by generating a list of three things for which you are grateful. Many people report that it is more effective if you write your gratitude list. So use your Gratitude Journal daily to recall what made you feel happy, lucky, grateful, or blessed. This simple exercise redirects your focus, banishing resentment. You become a happier person almost effortlessly. And among other benefits, grateful, happy people cope better with anger. You'll also discover that you unconsciously start seeking out and paying more attention to the parts of your day that you know you can feel grateful for. Gratitude begets gratitude.

SAMPLE GRATITUDE JOURNAL ENTRIES:

Sunday:

- *I'm grateful for my daughter's smile.*
- *I enjoyed my first cup of coffee this morning.*
- *I had fun on my lunch break with my co-worker, Lisa.*

Monday:

- *Today I saw the sweetest little goldfinch outside my window.*
- *I was early to work and had time to read the newspaper.*
- *My friend called to say hello, and we had a nice chat this afternoon.*

Tuesday:

- *I ordered the chocolate cake for dessert at dinner, and it was delicious.*
- *I had just enough time to call Maggie for a walk after work and the weather was perfect.*
- *My mom got good news about her medical test.*

EXERCISE 33: YOUR GRATITUDE JOURNAL

As you keep a Gratitude Journal, track its effectiveness by completing your Anger Tracking Chart. Watch how your anger levels drop when you're maintaining a grateful outlook.

	Sun	Mon	Tues	Wed	Thurs	Fri	Sat
Journal							
Intense Anger							
Moderate Anger							
Mild Anger							
Calm							

◈ URGENT CARE PRAYER

An Urgent Care Prayer is exactly what it sounds like: a prayer you call upon in an anger crisis. Urgent Care Prayers remind us of our true goals, our broader plans, and our overall spiritual objectives. A simple example of such a prayer is I pray for love and not hate, kindness and not anger, forgiveness and not blame.

If you are familiar with your own anger patterns, triggers, and tendencies, then you will know when anger is on the horizon. You can have your own Urgent Care Prayer ready for the next opportunity to manage anger. After you've written your own Urgent Care Prayer, recite it twice a day for the next week. The next time you find yourself in the midst of anger, stop and instantly recite your Urgent Care Prayer in your mind. Say the prayer to yourself at least twice—more, if necessary—as a way to realign your mind with your higher intentions.

One way to train for sudden moments of anger is to recite your Urgent Care Prayer even when you're feeling calm and happy. The more you internalize your prayer, the more likely you are to access it during an angry moment and to prevent relapse.

YOUR SUPPORT CIRCLE

Another aspect of life balance is your social support: family, friends, co-workers, neighbors, and any professional "helpers" in your life. These are people who make up your team, who can assist you during times of need, share your happiness during times of joy, calm you down when you are feeling angry, encourage you during times of stress, reassure you when you are feeling worried, and offer you new perspectives when you are feeling stuck.

Often, we forget that there are people who can help or we turn to the wrong people. If you are feeling alone or disconnected, remember your support circle and reach out to them! See the ***Jumpstart Exercise to help complete your own.***

EXERCISE 34: YOUR SUPPORT INVENTORY

It is essential to take stock of your social network so that you will know whom to call on in different situations. This exercise helps you evaluate your current support circle, clarifying how each relationship offers a differing type and level of support and helping you pinpoint the relationships that are most helpful, particularly in managing anger.

1. Who is the person I trust the most with my innermost thoughts and feelings?

2. Who makes me feel loved and understood?

3. To whom do I feel closest?

4. Who is the person who is most reliably willing to return my calls?

5. Who is the person who best helps me to calm down when angry?

6. Who is the person in my life who is the most encouraging and optimistic?

7. Who is the person I can go to when I need to find a fresh perspective?

8. Who is the person I can go to when I need to be distracted from my own ruminations and anxieties?

9. Who are the people who are "in and out" (variable) in regard to their availability or willingness to offer support?

10. Who is the person in my life who is "up for anything" and is almost always ready to make a light, fun social plan?

11. Who are my most "distant" friends?

12. Who are the people in my life whom I enjoy socially, but whom I don't feel ready to let in on my deepest thoughts, feelings, and fears?

YOUR SUPPORT CIRCLE

Now that you have done your inventory, plot your support system visually on the graph below. Who is in your innermost circle? Who is only sometimes there and only sometimes helpful—on the circle's middle ring? Who is on the outer periphery? Look at your friend and family to see which people will be your best bets when it comes time to seek support. See the *Jumpstart Exercise to help you complete your support circle.*

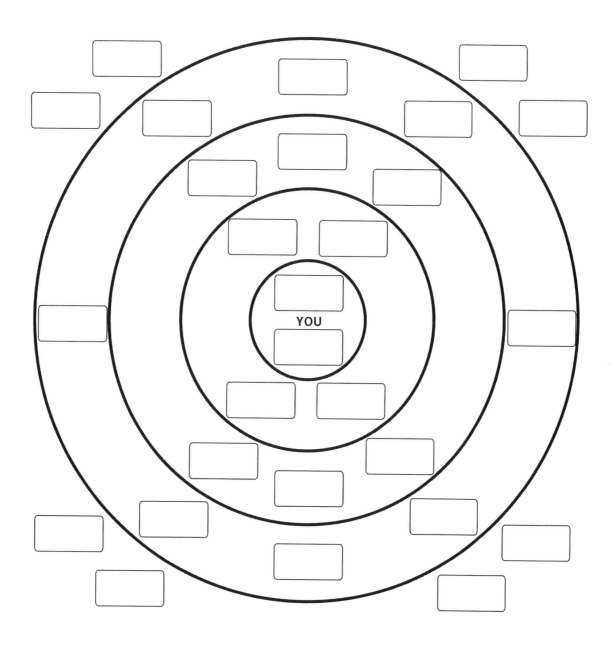

Jumpstart the Exercise: Bob's example

1. Who is the person I trust the most with my innermost thoughts and feelings? *My girlfriend, Sue*

2. Who makes me feel loved and understood? *My girlfriend, Sue*

3. To whom do I feel closest? *Sue, Mom, and Dave sometimes*

4. Who is the person who is most reliably willing to return my calls? *Sue and Mom*

5. Who is the person who best helps me to calm down when I'm angry? *Dave, Steve, Megan*

6. Who is the person in my life who is the most encouraging and optimistic? *Mom*

7. Who is the person I can go to when I need to find a fresh perspective? *Dave mostly, but also my old friend Carlos, my therapist Melissa, my former teacher Ms. J.*

8. Who is the person I can go to when I need to be distracted from my own ruminations and anxieties? *My co-worker Steve and my friend in California Megan*

9. Who are the people who are "in and out" (variable) in regard to their availability or willingness to offer support? *My stepdad, my aunt Deb, my neighbor Joe, ex-running buddy Michael, e-mail pen-pal Ned, childhood friend Ted, old roommate Dan, and my sister*

10. Who is the person in my life who is "up for anything" and is almost always ready to make a light, fun social plan? *Dave*

11. Who are my most "distant" friends? *John B., High School Buddies (Les, Bill, Wally), Jeanine, Uncle Gabe, Former Football teammates (Preston and Ralph)*

12. Who are the people in my life whom I enjoy socially, but whom I don't feel ready to let in on my deepest thoughts, feelings, and fears? *Co-worker Bethany, Neighbor Oscar, Church friend Alice, former co-worker Hal*

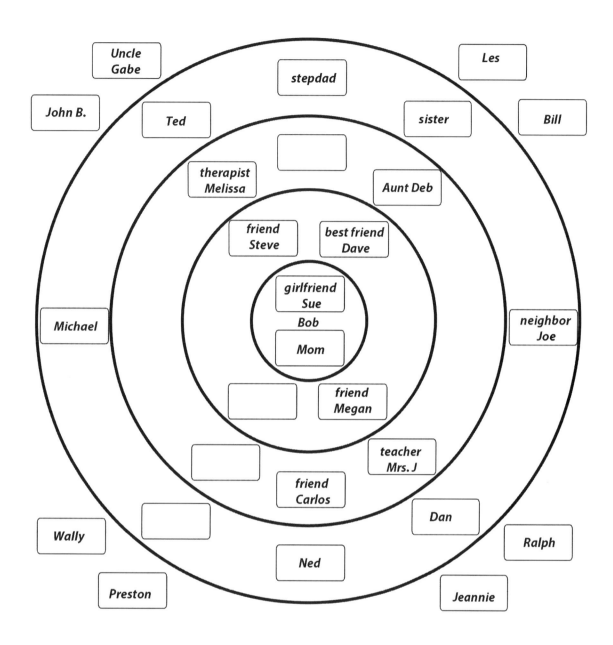

LIFE SATISFACTION ASSESSMENT

When you are more balanced and satisfied in most areas of your life, you will handle frustration and anger more confidently and calmly. Staying mindful of how satisfied you are will help keep you from slipping back into old anger patterns. So how would you rate your satisfaction? Think about family, career, spirituality, physical environment, finances, health, friendship, romance, education, and fun. Explore each category to better understand which areas are strong and which areas need improvement. See the ***Jumpstart Exercise to help you complete your life assessment.***

EXERCISE 35: YOUR LIFE ASSESSMENT

This exercise assesses the 10 central aspects of your life. It will help you identify areas where you can make changes and manage your frustration. I know how painful it can be to realize suddenly that your life is not at all what you yearn for it to be like. Keeping a log such as this over time will help you stay aware of how you are doing in the satisfaction department. The assessment is a tool that will help you discern quickly when changes occur and assist you to eliminate problems.

Use the scale below to rate your family satisfaction. Circle the number that best represents your level of satisfaction. If your satisfaction level is low, answer the following questions to explore how you might find more fulfillment. Then complete the remaining nine satisfaction categories the same way.

FAMILY

• 1 2 3 Range	• 4 5 6 Range	• 7 8 9 10 Range
Low Satisfaction	**Moderate Satisfaction**	**High Satisfaction**

1. What part of your family life is causing your dissatisfaction?

2. What is holding you back from having greater family satisfaction?

3. What needs to change in order to increase your family satisfaction to a moderate/high level?

CAREER

• 1 2 3 Range   • 4 5 6 Range   • 7 8 9 10 Range

Low Satisfaction   **Moderate Satisfaction**   **High Satisfaction**

1. What part of your career is causing your dissatisfaction?

2. What is holding you back from having greater career satisfaction?

3. What needs to change in order to increase your career satisfaction to a moderate/high level?

SPIRITUAL

• 1 2 3 Range   • 4 5 6 Range   • 7 8 9 10 Range

Low Satisfaction   **Moderate Satisfaction**   **High Satisfaction**

1. What part of your spiritual life is causing your dissatisfaction?

2. What is holding you back from having greater spiritual satisfaction?

3. What needs to change in order to increase your spiritual satisfaction to a moderate/high level?

HOME/PHYSICAL ENVIRONMENT

• 1 2 3 Range	• 4 5 6 Range	• 7 8 9 10 Range
Low Satisfaction	**Moderate Satisfaction**	**High Satisfaction**

1. What part of your home/physical environment is causing your dissatisfaction?

2. What is holding you back from having greater home/physical environment satisfaction?

3. What needs to change in order to increase your home/physical environment satisfaction to a moderate/high level?

MONEY

• 1 2 3 Range	• 4 5 6 Range	• 7 8 9 10 Range
Low Satisfaction	**Moderate Satisfaction**	**High Satisfaction**

1. What part of your financial life is causing your dissatisfaction?

2. What is holding you back from having greater financial satisfaction?

3. What needs to change in order to increase your financial satisfaction to a moderate/high level?

HEALTH

• 1 2 3 Range	• 4 5 6 Range	• 7 8 9 10 Range
Low Satisfaction	**Moderate Satisfaction**	**High Satisfaction**

1. What part of your health is causing your dissatisfaction?

2. What is holding you back from having greater health satisfaction?

3. What needs to change in order to increase your health satisfaction to a moderate/high level?

FRIENDSHIP

• 1 2 3 Range	• 4 5 6 Range	• 7 8 9 10 Range
Low Satisfaction	**Moderate Satisfaction**	**High Satisfaction**

1. What part of your friendship/social life is causing your dissatisfaction?

2. What is holding you back from having greater friendship/social satisfaction?

3. What needs to change in order to increase your friendship/social satisfaction to a moderate/high level?

ROMANCE

• 1 2 3 Range	• 4 5 6 Range	• 7 8 9 10 Range
Low Satisfaction	**Moderate Satisfaction**	**High Satisfaction**

1. What part of your romantic life is causing your dissatisfaction?

2. What is holding you back from having greater romantic satisfaction?

3. What needs to change in order to increase your romantic satisfaction to a moderate/high level?

EDUCATION/LEARNING

• 1 2 3 Range	• 4 5 6 Range	• 7 8 9 10 Range
Low Satisfaction	**Moderate Satisfaction**	**High Satisfaction**

1. What part of your education/learning is causing your dissatisfaction?

2. What is holding you back from having greater educational satisfaction?

3. What needs to change in order to increase your educational satisfaction to a moderate/high level?

FUN

• 1 2 3 Range	• 4 5 6 Range	• 7 8 9 10 Range
Low Satisfaction	**Moderate Satisfaction**	**High Satisfaction**

1. What part of your life in regard to fun is causing your dissatisfaction?

2. What is holding you back from having greater satisfaction in regard to fun?

3. What needs to change in order to increase your satisfaction in regard to fun to a moderate/high level?

Jumpstart the Exercise: Bob's Example

FAMILY
- 1 2 3 Range
- 4 5 **6** Range
- 7 8 9 10 Range

Low Satisfaction   **Moderate Satisfaction**   **High Satisfaction**

1. What part of your family life is causing your dissatisfaction?

    I wish I felt closer to my stepdad and sister.

2. What is holding you back from having greater family satisfaction?

    A feeling of awkwardness about the distance between me and my stepdad and sister.

3. What needs to change in order to increase your family satisfaction to a moderate/high level?

    I could be at the "High" level if I maintained the current good relationship with my mom, and then started to try to reach out more to my stepdad and sister. Maybe I could plan to spend more time with them.

CAREER
- 1 2 **3** Range
- 4 5 6 Range
- 7 8 9 10 Range

Low Satisfaction   **Moderate Satisfaction**   **High Satisfaction**

1. What part of your career is causing your dissatisfaction?

    I wish I made more money, and I'm trying to spend less time at work.

2. What is holding you back from having greater career satisfaction?

    The downturn at my job means I'm not making a lot of money right now. Also, I'm working on having more time for myself and for Sue. I spend too much time and energy on my job.

3. What needs to change in order to increase your career satisfaction to a moderate/high level?

    I need to gain confidence in my own value and promote it to my employer. I need to make sure my priorities are in line. I need to be more even-handed in the way I distribute my time.

SPIRITUAL
- 1 2 3 Range
- **4** 5 6 Range
- 7 8 9 10 Range

Low Satisfaction   **Moderate Satisfaction**   **High Satisfaction**

1. What part of your spiritual life is causing your dissatisfaction?

    My desire to be part of a spiritual community of people without going to a church or having to participate in organized religion.

2. What is holding you back from having greater spiritual satisfaction?

    A refusal to research other options for spiritual growth, a limited view of what it means to be spiritual.

3. What needs to change in order to increase your spiritual satisfaction to a moderate/high level?

    I need to expand my view of what spirituality might mean. I want to be more willing to go out and find people who can make me feel spiritually "at home" while also helping me grow spiritually.

HOME/PHYSICAL ENVIRONMENT

• 1 2 **3** Range	• 4 **5** 6 Range	• 7 8 9 10 Range
Low Satisfaction	**Moderate Satisfaction**	**High Satisfaction**

1. What part of your home/physical environment is causing your dissatisfaction?

   My home is small, and it embarrasses me.

2. What is holding you back from having greater home/physical environment satisfaction?

   My paycheck.

3. What needs to change in order to increase your home/physical environment satisfaction to a moderate/high level?

   I need to do two things: Save money for a larger home in the future, but also pay more attention to the positive aspects of the home I'm already in. It's small, so my utility bills are small, too. It's cozy, it's familiar, and it works for me.

MONEY

• **1** 2 3 Range	• 4 5 6 Range	• 7 8 9 10 Range
Low Satisfaction	**Moderate Satisfaction**	**High Satisfaction**

1. What part of your financial life is causing your dissatisfaction?

   I almost never feel like I'm financially successful enough.

2. What is holding you back from having greater financial satisfaction?

   My All-or-Nothing Thinking, fear of inadequacy, and magnified focus on money as worth.

3. What needs to change in order to increase your financial satisfaction to a moderate/high level?

   I want to change the way I think about money and self-worth. I want to be more grateful for the fact that I'm employed, that I have a paycheck, and that I pay all of my bills on time. I want to let go of the unhealthy notion that my finances define who I am and whether I can be happy in life.

HEALTH

• 1 2 3 Range	•4 5 6 Range	• **7** 8 9 10 Range
Low Satisfaction	**Moderate Satisfaction**	**High Satisfaction**

1. What part of your health is causing your dissatisfaction?

   Not much really, but I guess there's always room for improvement.

2. What is holding you back from having greater health satisfaction?

   I guess I could exercise more if I worked less.

3. What needs to change in order to increase your health satisfaction to a moderate/high level?

   I could add some more exercise into my routine. But I'm a pretty fit, healthy guy overall anyway.

FRIENDS

• 1 2 3 Range	• 4 5 **6** Range	• 7 8 9 10 Range
Low Satisfaction	**Moderate Satisfaction**	**High Satisfaction**

1. What part of your friendship/social life is causing your dissatisfaction?

   I could stand to have at least one or two more CLOSE friends.

2. What is holding you back from having greater friendship/social satisfaction?

   I rely almost exclusively on Sue, Dave, and my mom. I am resistant to making new friends.

3. What needs to change in order to increase your friendship/social satisfaction to a moderate/high level?

   If I worked even slightly less, I could have more time to go out socially and make new friends. I could also focus on nurturing and growing some of my existing friendships.

ROMANCE

• 1 2 3 Range	• 4 5 6 Range	• 7 **8** 9 10 Range
Low Satisfaction	**Moderate Satisfaction**	**High Satisfaction**

1. What part of your romantic life is causing your dissatisfaction?

   Just my jealousy and fear. Otherwise, our relationship is excellent.

2. What is holding you back from having greater romantic satisfaction?

   My unwillingness to trust and be open.

3. What needs to change in order to increase your romantic satisfaction to a moderate/high level?

   I need to look at the facts without Assuming the Worst or Catastrophizing. I need to let myself be loved. I need to work on trusting my girlfriend and trusting myself to cope if something goes wrong.

EDUCATION/LEARNING

• 1 2 **3** Range	• 4 5 6 Range	• 7 8 9 10 Range
Low Satisfaction	**Moderate Satisfaction**	**High Satisfaction**

1. What part of your education/learning is causing your dissatisfaction?

   I want to learn Spanish.

2. What is holding you back from having greater educational satisfaction?

   I keep making excuses about not having enough time.

3. What needs to change in order to increase your educational satisfaction to a moderate/high level?

   Less work, less time on the iPhone, and so on. If I cut a couple of useless activities, I would have plenty of time to learn Spanish.

FUN

• 1 2 3 Range	• 4 5 6 Range	• 7 8 9 10 Range
Low Satisfaction	**Moderate Satisfaction**	**High Satisfaction**

1. What part of your life in regard to "fun" is causing your dissatisfaction?

   I work too much.

2. What is holding you back from having greater satisfaction in regard to "fun"?

   My priorities and insecurities.

3. What needs to change in order to increase your satisfaction in regard to "fun" to a moderate/high level?

   I need to take a hard look at my life and remember what matters most. I want to have fun and spend time enjoying my life, not just always working.

LIFE SATISFACTION

As an adult, you may have lost sight of many of the very things that make you feel most happy and satisfied. The more satisfied you are with your life, the better you can manage anger. One way to create a strong, satisfied sense of self is to find what you enjoy doing and do more of it. Hobbies, interests, and pleasures are not just for fun—they're an important part of self-care. Better self-care leads to lowered stress, overall satisfaction, and improved temper taming and relapse prevention.

EXERCISE 36: YOUR SATISFACTION CHEAT SHEET

Start by listing your likes and dislikes. Come up with activities that reflect those likes and dislikes. This exercise might help prompt you to remember things you like to do that you neglected or ignored for years. When you reacquaint yourself with your own preferences, it gives you the chance to boost your overall life satisfaction.

WHAT I LIKE	ACTIVITIES TO ADD	WHAT I DISLIKE	ACTIVITIES TO AVOID
Sunshine	Going for a walk	Cold Weather	Skiing, Ice Skating
Music	Playing piano	Long lines	Saturday at the mall

Start doing three activities from the "What I like" list more often. Take three items from the "What I dislike" list and stop doing them or at least do them less often. Even slight shifts in either direction will improve your life balance and satisfaction. Every six months or so, revisit your list and revise it as your needs and desires change.

Conclusion

I think of my client Edward as a poster child for temper taming. He graduated from the Naval Academy and had a brilliant naval career before joining the private sector as the CEO of a major furniture company. He first came to me because he was unhappy in his job but felt trapped. He was making a lot of money, but his job didn't seem to provide much pleasure.

Edward treated his employees like they weren't human beings. One of his triggers is ignorance, so if he told employees how to do their job, and they kept asking the same questions, that set him off. He would hold staff meetings and blast them all, shouting and cursing "I'll fire you all, if you don't turn yourself around in two weeks." He had no empathy or tolerance for what he perceived as laziness. He was also taking out all this frustration, stress, and anger on his wife and three kids. He acted like a dictator at home, using profanity, and exploding verbally.

When Edward first started seeing me, he seemed depressed as well as angry. I soon discovered that two years ago, he'd lost his mom who had been his primary emotional support. They used to talk all the time, and Edward was having tremendous trouble adjusting to the loss. He hadn't done any grief work yet. I thought, okay, there's the pain that's usually hiding under anger.

I started helping him understand his grief, and then I moved on to attacking his anger. Edward had to learn the difference between discipline and punishment when it came to his children. He had to learn to focus on the employees' positive performance and remain calm and patient with those struggling with their jobs. By taking the step to admit that he had an anger problem, he committed to learning about anger. He takes frequent time-outs and uses the other tools from this book every day. Today, Edward is much calmer and happier.

Edward tamed his temper, and so can you.

Congratulations for setting aside time and space to overcome aggression. This workbook is not the end of dealing with your anger, of course. It is only the beginning. I know you will become angry again and that someone will be angry with you. Your heart will race, your thoughts will change, and your feelings will swell—again. But it won't be the same old same old. Now you understand where anger comes from, what causes it, and what you can do about it. You have tools to manage your anger. The good news is that the concepts in this book will work if you implement them.

Made in the USA
San Bernardino, CA
17 November 2013